D0344485

Fishing for Barracuda

PRAGMATICS OF BRIEF SYSTEMIC THERAPY

A NORTON PROFESSIONAL BOOK

Fishing for Barracuda

PRAGMATICS OF BRIEF SYSTEMIC THERAPY

Joel S. Bergman

W · W · NORTON & COMPANY

New York   *London*

Published simultaneously in Canada by Penguin Books Canada Ltd,
2801 John Street, Markham, Ontario L3R 1B4

Printed in the United States of America.

First Edition

Library of Congress Cataloging in Publication Data

Bergman, Joel S.
  Fishing for barracuda.

  Bibliography: p.
  Includes indexes.
  1. Psychotherapy, Brief. 2. Family psychotherapy.
3. Resistance (Psychoanalysis) I. Title.
RC480.55.B47   1985   616.89′14   84-29494

ISBN 0-393-70005-4

W. W. Norton & Company, Inc., 500 Fifth Avenue, New York, N.Y. 10110

W. W. Norton & Company Ltd., 37 Great Russell Street, London WC1B 3NU

1 2 3 4 5 6 7 8 9 0

*"What is of all things most yielding,
can overcome that which is most hard."*

*"That the yielding conquers the resistant
and the soft conquers the hard
is a fact known by all men,
yet utilized by none..."*

Lao Tzu

CONTENTS

FOREWORD

Mara Selvini Palazzoli

I first met Joel in October 1977 at the Ackerman Institute in New York, where I went, with Giuliana Prata and my former associates, Luigi Boscolo and Gianfranco Cecchin, to present for the first time to an American audience our way of working with families. Turning over the pages of the little notebook in which at that time I diligently wrote, day by day, the events of that journey, I discover, to my surprise, that in the afternoon of October 13, "A young man named Joel Bergman is courageous enough to be the first to expose himself conducting a session with a family of a chronic agoraphobic patient." This awakens memories, and I see in a flashback a nice youth who gave me the impression of being very gifted and deeply convinced of the importance of what he was doing. His book now confirms all my first impressions.

It is not an easy choice to opt for the treatment of the most impervious families! As the author sharply emphasizes (using the metaphor of the encounter of the fisherman with the barracuda), the therapist will succeed only if he is free of two fears: that of the bites of the "beast" and that of missing the target. This certainly does not mean that one can improvise, counting only on one's own personal qualities. A rigorous procedure is a must. So in the first chapter the author underlines the importance of considering in detail many problems: the referring person, certain revealing characteristics of the first telephone call, the level of discomfort and anxiety in the fami-

ix

ly and its disposition to submit to the rules of the therapist. Moreover, he insists, the therapist has to be rigorous in defining the asymmetry of the therapeutic relationship and therefore his right to decide who must come to the session.

Most of all, Joel rightly points out that live supervision is indispensable. Chapter 4 on *Use and Abuse of Teams* was for me really fascinating and provoked an exciting discussion here at the Nuovo Centro: What is the ideal number of the components of a team in the different phases of its evolution? Could a team really be overskilled for a certain situation in a family, or does the overskillfulness consist only in confusing complication with complexity?

In the last pages of Joel's inspiring book I felt a bit of weariness, of discouragement. He mentions Bateson's famous statement concerning his experience with schizophrenics, as quoted by Laing, "I am fed up with their dumb cruelty." I myself (I clearly remember) was struck and hurt when I read that sentence, and for some time I felt miserable. But, stubborn as I am, I quickly decided that the fault was not in the families but in the tools I used with them. So I had to search and search to find out something *completely* different. Who stops gets lost. Go ahead, Joel!

Milan, February 1985

ACKNOWLEDGMENTS

My first mentor was Kitty LaPerriere, who was the Director of Training when I started my training at the Ackerman Institute for Family Therapy in 1974. That year Kitty taught me many things, but two things stand out most in my mind and continue to influence my work. First, one day, while I was trying to get my left hemisphere to understand what my right hemisphere knew, Kitty said that the best I could do would be to develop a comfortable exchange between the two hemispheres and leave it at that, because one will never completely "understand" the other. Second, Kitty, like all great teachers, taught by "giving permission" for me to use my unrecognized and unknown strengths and talents. There was no rigid, dogmatic, "this is the only way to do therapy" stance. Her quiet confidence in permitting me to develop my own resources to do treatment will always be important to me.

Two other important mentors were Olga Silverstein and Peggy Papp, who were co-directors of the Brief Therapy Project for the four or five years I was associated with that project. Peggy also taught by giving permission—permission to experiment, to use humor and playfulness and, as a brief systemic therapist, to take full responsibility for change. When a family didn't change, we assumed that we had formulated the wrong hypothesis or intervention rather than blame the family or couple for being impossibly resistant.

If Kitty permitted me to have a comfortable exchange between my left and right hemisphere, Olga permitted me to have no left hemisphere at all, and for that I will always be grateful.

I would like to thank Donald Bloch, Director of the Ackerman Institute for Family Therapy, for encouraging the Brief Therapy Project and for always permitting experimentation and diversity. The Ackerman Institute provided a wonderful opportunity to work with and learn from a talented and innovative faculty.

I would like to thank Ian Alger, who when he wasn't being my therapist served as a wonderful model for the use of humor, metaphor, outrageousness, aliveness and playfulness. Because I love and respect Ian, he gave me permission to use these qualities in my own work.

Gillian Walker, my big sister, cotherapist and teammate for eight years, gave me the validation and confidence that I was special and that some of the things I was doing in treatment were not being done by everyone else. Gillian is the colleague I go to when I'm stuck; every family therapist should be blessed with such a lifeguard.

I would like to thank Susan E. Barrows, Director of Norton Professional Books, for her confidence in me, her gentle editorial comments and suggestions, and her courage in letting me write this book in my own style. I am also grateful to Michael Berger and Kitty La Perriere for reading the manuscript and making helpful comments and recommendations.

Finally, I would like to thank my parents, Eleanor and Max Bergman. Without them, this book would never have been written.

Joel S. Bergman, Ph.D.
March, 1985

PREFACE

I was in Eilat, Israel, about to do some snorkeling in the beautiful Red Sea, and I asked a local Israeli if it was dangerous to swim in these waters. He told me that it was pretty safe—except for the poisonous coral, which I should not touch, and of course, the barracuda.

"Will the barracuda attack me?"

"Only if you scare them," replied the Israeli.

"What will scare them?"

"If you show panic," he said with a smile. So the only way I could snorkel in the Red Sea would be to show controlled terror in the event a barracuda came along.

This is exactly what happened. A barracuda came along and gently nudged my facemask. Frozen in terror, I started to smile inside as I thought, "How do you nonverbally show a barracuda that you are not afraid—and if you are able to show this nonchalance, would it be insulting to the barracuda?" I amused myself with these obsessive questions, in my frozen state of terror—and I suspect quite frankly that I became rather boring to the barracuda. Whatever the reason, he or she moved on.

There are many reasons why this book is entitled as it is. I have used "barracuda" as a metaphor in the title of some training workshops and conferences, and clinicians seem to understand and enjoy the metaphor. I think clinicians appreciate the implication of the potential lethality in working with some of these families to the health and welfare of the clinician. So much has been written on these families, and so little on the danger of treating these families to the clinician. One of the goals of this book is to help the clinician change these families while surviving and staying alive as a therapist.

It is important to emphasize that the potential lethality and ferocity of such families have more to do with fusion than with resistance. I see clinicians struggling with the family's perceived terror of what will happen to them (the family) if and when a family member separates and becomes somewhat emotionally independent of the family. Clearly, it is easier to emotionally leave some families than others. When clinicians choose to treat those families less "generous" with separation and differentiation, they will invariably experience what Murray Bowen (1978) has always informally and respectfully described as "fusion raising its ugly head." It's the rage, terror, anxiety, panic – the intense emotionality that is concomitant to these emotional separations – which makes the therapy difficult.

For those who enjoy fishing as a sport, there is another metaphor inherent in the title. Fishing is basically a tranquil, relaxing, peaceful sport – requiring thought and patience. The interesting thing about fishing for me is the extreme and sudden polarity – going from a calm, tranquil, serene state to sudden struggle, violence, and drama when a fish bites the hook. Like working with families, fishing can be an experience of quick, dramatic changes.

Fishing for Barracuda also implies a contest between the barracuda and the fisherman. The barracuda is quick, smart, lethal and "skilled" at being a barracuda. Fishermen must be experienced and skilled in catching barracuda, and the contest between the two must be close. Another goal of this book is to share with fishermen still interested in barracuda some thoughts and techniques which might increase their skills.

I have been doing brief systemic therapy for the past 10 years. In fact, I don't think I know how to do long–term treatment. My training began in the Brief Therapy Project at the Ackerman Institute in 1975, and I have continued to do brief therapy ever since, both at the Institute and in my private practice.

My posture towards psychotherapy and towards myself as a therapist is to see what I do as emergency road service. I assume that people and families come into treatment because they are stuck somewhere on their own roads. They have tried to solve their problems by themselves and have not been able to do so. They are also somewhat demoralized because their attempted solutions have failed. My job is to get these people back on the road as quickly as possible. As I tell my patients, I do not do tuneups, overhauls, or bodywork – I just do whatever is needed to get that car back on the road. If people want more after that, I will refer them to specialists who do tuneups, overhauls, or bodywork. Occasionally, I do overhauls myself, based upon a request and my agreement at the outset of therapy, but my basic posture as a therapist is to get people out of therapy as quickly as possible.

In part, this thinking is based upon my view of people as pretty good problem-solvers. What often happens is that people get stuck in their own emotionality or the fusion in their own family systems and attempt unsuccessfully to solve their problems using first-order solutions. Often the solution to a particular problem is to talk with someone who is *outside* or *meta* to the emotionality or fusion in an individual's system. A sufficiently skilled person who is meta to this system can devise a second-order solution to the presenting problem. Once this second-order solution is attempted and the family or patient gets "unstuck," the car can get back on the road and do all right.

What I find interesting as I continue to learn about doing psychotherapy is how often there is just one puzzle; when my hypothesis is correct and the ritual I devise to solve this puzzle is delivered correctly, change takes place very quickly. And often, once the puzzle or riddle is solved, the person and family can get on without much more help. If an individual or family wants more therapy, this can be arranged, but it is different from resolving that one presenting puzzle.

I enjoy the problem-solving part of the therapy – finding the solution to the riddle or the puzzle. That intellectual activity keeps me interested in the field. To continue to remain interested in this field, I need to find briefer and more effective ways of solving problems.

Sometimes my families ask, "How brief is brief?" My answer is, "Less time than usual." "Well, how long is usual?" "Well, that depends on how motivated you are in wanting change, how fast you will work and do your homework." One of the nicest things about doing brief systemic therapy is that people can't con you on how much they want to change. If they say they want to change, and you give them assignments, homework, and rituals, and they wind up not being able to do them, you can argue that they don't want to change *that much* (or it was the "wrong" homework or formulation). One patient, a baker, remarked, "One of the nice things about working in concrete ways [as in doing homework and rituals] is that it minimizes nonsense. Either you do something or you don't. You know how to make a good croissant or you don't." You do the ritual or you don't.

I think with pride of the briefest case I ever had. This involved never seeing the family, only giving the family a ritual over the phone – with no charge, of course. For me that was the most elegant piece of work I have done, and I hope to have more opportunities to work this way. It's no way to make a living, but it certainly is a way of staying alive.

Another reason for writing this book comes from where I am presently in my personal and professional life cycle. Becoming a family therapist and a specialist in treating resistant families was an attempt on my part to understand my own situation and to individuate from my family. My relationship with my nuclear and extended families is quite different today from what it was 10 years ago; consequently, my interest in family therapy has changed. I have learned a lot about families, and this book is an attempt to share some of the things I have learned about resistance, as well as about change.

These days, I am less interested in barracuda – chronic schizophrenics or resistant families who have defeated other professionals. For one thing, I have become less tolerant (from my perspective) of the cruelty displayed in these families.

Secondly, once you slay a few dragons, the dragons no longer become challenging, scary, and for that matter interesting. What presently interests me is writing a fishing manual on barracuda and other game and editing training videotapes on the process of changing couples and families. I am currently writing about therapeutic rituals used in couple and individual therapy.

I will probably continue to be a family therapist, because I like families and couples and because I like and need to solve problems. What will change is the level of nastiness and cruelty in the more difficult families, of which I am less tolerant, because I am less tolerant of experiencing these qualities in my own family. I hope that this new intolerance will be a step toward emotionally growing up, having less need to please others, and being less competitively reactive to the challenges which these difficult families present.

Fishing for Barracuda

PRAGMATICS OF
BRIEF SYSTEMIC
THERAPY

1

SELECTING
RESISTANT FAMILIES

The issues facing a clinician who is about to treat a "resist-ant" family are similar to many of the issues involved in see-ing a "cooperative" family. However, additional factors and issues must be considered when a difficult family is seeking treatment. This chapter discusses some of these added fac-tors and shows how to: recognize resistant families; obtain critical information during the initial telephone conversation; recognize friendly and unfriendly referrals; gauge resistance; determine which family members will be invited to the first session; and deal with pre-first-session maneuvers.

CHARACTERISTICS OF RESISTANT FAMILIES

My definition of a difficult or resistant family is *one which has demonstrated an impressive history of defeating mental health professionals.* The impressiveness of the family's his-tory could take the form of defeating prestigious training in-stitutes or therapists or having a long history (five or more years) of defeating many therapists.

Once I learn from the initial telephone conversation about this impressive history of treatment failure, I immediately begin thinking in my "resistance mode" and seeing the family differently from the way I would see a less resistant family. (I might add that resistant families are far from resistant throughout the entire course of therapy. Often after initial

3

resistance is reduced and the family is "captured" [see Chapter 2] one can go about treating the family members as if they were cooperative until new resistance is met by the clinician. Basically, I do structural family therapy with most families until I encounter resistance, whereupon I usually deal with the resistance in some brief systemic way.)

Another way in which I gauge the family's resistance comes from a description of the symptom. *Usually, the more severe and chronic the symptom, the more resistant the family will be to change.* This hypothesis is based upon my clinical experiences with resistant families, which have led to some working assumptions, such as:

1) All symptoms in children stabilize unstable marriages, and if a "small" symptom cannot stabilize a marriage, then a "larger" symptom is needed.
2) The greater the magnitude of the marital conflict, the greater will be the magnitude of the symptom.
3) The more covert or hidden the marital conflict, the more a symptom will be needed to stabilize the marital conflict so it can remain hidden or covert.

My assumption that all symptoms stabilize unstable marriages comes from my clinical experience working with symptomatic children. In *every* case treated over the past 10 years, the elimination of a child's symptom has been accompanied by an intensification and magnification of a marital conflict. In addition, once the marital conflict is overt, acknowledged, and addressed by the couple in therapy, the symptomatic child seldom remains symptomatic. When the couple does not acknowledge the problem or is not willing to address it in treatment, then the child's symptom is maintained either periodically or continuously.

After the symptom in the child has been eliminated, I *never* begin marital therapy with the child's parents until the couple directly makes that request. Doing couple work before the spouses are ready to work often results in the child "rescuing" them by producing symptoms again. Then the couple will use marital therapy only to talk about their symptomatic child. Therefore, the clinician must wait until the child's symptom is eliminated, *followed* by a request by the couple for marital work. Sometimes the request never comes because the parents stabilize their system with something other than the child's symptom, such as another psychotherapist, another child or another symptom in the same child, a lover, alcohol, work, etc. Sometimes the partners work out the problem on their own.

Over the years, however, the seesaw relationship I have observed between a child's symptom and a marital conflict has convinced me that all symptoms in children stabilize marriages.

Experience has also taught me that the more severe and chronic the symptom, the more resistant the family will be to change. When family members with a chronic problem come to me and unfold an impressive history of treatment failure, they are telling me something. I assume that some of the therapists that the family has defeated are well trained; therefore, a chronic history tells me that the family is looking for homeostasis rather than change and will be resistant.

A severe symptom also tells me that the system will resist change because it requires such a "big" symptom to stabilize it. I assume that in all family systems "little" symptoms probably occur first, and if a small symptom is not sufficient to stabilize a system, a larger one will develop. Further evidence for this assumption occurs when I am able to eliminate the symptom in a family. When the severe, chronic symptom is eliminated, the resulting systems change, particularly in the marital pair, is more drastic than when the symptom is small. For example, with psychosis or anorexia, elimination of the symptom may result in divorce, abandonment, severe depression or illness, and sometimes a death, such as in suicide. Eliminating a small symptom, such as bed-wetting, acting-out in school, or discipline problems, often results in less drastic marital reactions.

My last assumption is that *the more covert or hidden the marital conflict, the more a symptom will be needed to stabilize the conflict so it can remain hidden or covert.* In general I have found that the more fighting there is between the partners, or the more overt the couple's conflicts are, the easier it is to help the family system change. When partners tell me that they have never fought or have never had differences in their 25-year marriage, I get very anxious, because I suspect a furious covert war is going on, which would lead to very resistant symptoms in the children, or to murder, suicide, or serious illness in the couple. The more overt fighting and conflict between the couple, the more opportunities there will be for me as a clinician to facilitate change.

Therefore, my assumptions about treating a resistant family with an anorectic, bulimic, schizophrenic, manic-depressive, or hospitalized obsessive-compulsive are quite different from my assumptions about treating a family when the presenting problem is bed-wetting or a mild behavior disorder. In the former group, I assume that an intense, often covert marital conflict is present and that there will be considerable resistance to treatment because of the family's fear (real or imagined) that if treatment were to be successful someone (usually one of the parents) would leave (divorce, become seriously ill, or die). In the case of the bed-wetter, I assume a less intense and/or more overt marital conflict, where the family system is in less jeopardy if and when a symptom is eliminated.

Another index I often use to determine the degree of resistance in a system is the number of other psychotherapists currently associated with a family. These other therapists I jokingly refer to as Drs. Homeostat. My experience suggests that the greater the number of Drs. Homeostat involved with the case, the more the family will be resistant to change. Not only do families use Drs. Homeostat in their attempts to stabilize a family system, but sometimes these very homeostats serve almost iatrogenic functions. Therefore, they are one of the first factors to consider and eliminate so that one can begin to deal with the nuclear family system.

I am reminded of a case I treated a few years ago in the Brief Therapy Project at the Ackerman Institute for Family Therapy. The patient was a 30-year-old male who had been in and out of hospitals for the past nine years with a diagnosis of manic-depressive disorder. The patient was first hospitalized at the age of 19, at which time he was treated in the hospital by a young resident in biological psychiatry. Ten years later, we learned that this biological psychiatrist had become the family's psychiatrist, not only prescribing medication for the patient, but also giving antidepressant medication and electroconvulsive shock treatment to the patient's father and prescribing Valium for his mother. Whenever mother would become anxious about her son or husband, she would call Dr. Homeostat for some change in the medication being prescribed for her men.

Early in the treatment of this family it became clear that this doctor was a close, important member of this family. It was as if this doctor was another son in this family, as if the doctor and the son did parallel residencies, the former in biological psychiatry and the latter in manic-depressive psychosis.

As we began treatment, I did not take this Dr. Homeostat into account the way I would today. Whenever treatment started to shift the family system, someone, usually the mother, would get Dr. Homeostat to change someone's medication. Almost every therapeutic shift produced a biologically oriented or psychiatric countershift, and very little headway was made in treatment. In retrospect, if I had to treat this family today, knowing how important this Dr. Homeostat and the biological medication were to them, I would not start the treatment without including Dr.

Homeostat in at least the first or early sessions. That way, I could get a fix on how his position in the family stabilized the system and prevented it from changing in what I would call therapeutic directions.*

* * * *

I am further reminded of a phone conversation I once had with a woman who called and asked me to do a consultation with her family. The woman, her husband and her two sons, the latter two being the identified patients, had all been in individual therapy for many years. She was calling me because, although the family was presently in family therapy too, she was unhappy with the progress and wanted another opinion.

My opinion was that she was not giving all these therapists a fair chance. I said that after she had given all these therapists a fair shake, and had terminated all treatments, and was *still* unhappy, then I would be happy to see the family for a consultation. It was clear to me over the phone that this woman was not looking for a consultation, but merely another Dr. Homeostat to stabilize a system, probably because one of the many therapists involved with this case had started to change the family system. Now,

---

*About four years after I ended treatment with the family, the patient was hospitalized again and the family sought family therapy from the hospital. The family therapist at this hospital happened to be one of the students taking a course I was teaching at the Ackerman Institute entitled "Treating Resistant Families." When the family told my student that they had been in treatment at Ackerman, my student asked me whether I knew the family. To make matters more ironic, the student wanted to bring this family to the class at the Institute for treatment in order to get more out of the course. We decided that the family again was looking for homeostasis rather than change, and that the only way in which the family would be able to be treated at this hospital by this student would be under my supervision. When the family was told this, they decided that family therapy was not necessarily in their best interests. I interpreted this to mean that the family preferred maintaining homeostasis with a student therapist rather than risking change with the student's teacher.

I am certainly invested in helping families change, but I am not interested in having my toes munched on by barracuda.

Another determinant of resistance will briefly be mentioned here and discussed in greater detail later in this chapter. This has to do with the referral process or the context in which a family is referred for treatment. Sometimes, for example, one finds resistance against change inherent more in the referring context than in the family. The referral might be a "setup" for failure, as could occur when one receives an "unfriendly" referral. Before treatment can be initiated in such a situation, potential sources of resistance in the referring context must be evaluated and reduced or eliminated.

Other sources of resistance can be determined over the telephone during the initial phone conversation with the family. Since treatment begins with the initial phone call, the way in which information is collected and resistance handled during this conversation is an essential part of treatment.

THE INITIAL PHONE CALL

Whether the family calls me directly, or a referring therapist calls me, or I receive an intake form from a clinician who has had some phone contact with the family, the initial phone interview I do is pretty much the same. Although I consider clinical information gathered by other professionals, I do not study it too carefully, since I prefer my own biases to those of other professionals. Often, I have found that even historical information about a family is inaccurately obtained by other professionals or has not been offered by the family, so I usually take what is shared by other professionals in a tentative way.

My first contact with the family is a phone call to the person who initially called. During the call one of the first things I do is sketch a rough genogram that includes all members of the nuclear family with their ages, marital status, and whereabouts. I also look for "significant others" living in the household and keep an eye out for grandparents or other significant third-generation people living upstairs or close by. These are important because one of the recurring themes in resistant families with a severe symptom is unfinished business that parents have with *their* parents, which keeps the identified patient (IP) in the third generation from emotionally growing up and leaving home.

After collecting the information for this rough family genogram, I obtain a history of the symptomatology. In my mind, the more chronic the symptom appears to be, the more difficult the family therapy will be and the more resistant the family system will be to change. A brief history of treatment is also obtained. As mentioned above, an impressive history of treatment failures tells me that the family may be more adept and experienced at staying the same and resisting treatment than I am at changing the family patterns.

I then begin thinking about whether I will see this family alone, with a cotherapist, or with a team of family therapists observing behind a one-way mirror. If a family's history appears overwhelming, I usually think about inviting a cotherapist to join me in the treatment. After the initial session with a cotherapist, I can then decide whether a team is also necessary. My experience with difficult families suggests that the more resistant, difficult, and tricky the family is, the more I need additional therapeutic people on hand. How many therapists are needed to deal with these families varies with the family and the experience of the family therapist(s). It is important that the therapeutic force *for* change matches or is greater than the family force *against* change.

I was presenting an edited videotape of family therapy with a chronic agoraphobic at a conference attended by psychoanalysts (Bergman, 1981a). I was working with a team, and making the point that we, the therapists, gave the family a powerful mixed message—the therapist saying "change," but the team pointing out the dangers of changing. This therapeutic mixed message was necessary to match or be symmetrical with the family's mixed message of "help us change, but don't change us." The actual case is described elsewhere (Bergman & Walker, 1983).

I was trying to explain to the audience how the therapeutic message had to match the family's message both in power and in mixed messages. A member of the audience then suggested that the best way to counter the family's mixed message might be to have a matched therapeutic family (namely, the team), which would come up with a therapeutic message which would be equal to or more powerful than the family's messages. In other words, the therapeutic family would be matched in number of family members and experience in order to develop therapeutic messages for change more powerful than the clinical family's messages against change.

I suspect that over time and with experience clinicians become more able to gauge how much therapeutic force is needed. When working with these families, it is clearly to the clinician's advantage to have available as many therapeutic combinations as possible. It is also to the experienced clinician's advantage to know when more therapeutic force is needed. Many times, less experienced therapists find themselves in hot water when they realize, often too late, that the family system is more powerful than the therapeutic system. It is very difficult for a therapist to drop a family from treatment in the fourth session, after the therapist realizes that the family is more powerful than the therapist. When such dropping occurs, the experience can be quite demoralizing to the family (Bergman & Walker, 1983).

How does one train an inexperienced therapist to gauge how much therapeutic power is needed to treat certain families? I'm not sure. Many therapists learn this retrospectively, by being "done in" enough times to appreciate the limitations of their power as a solo therapist. Perhaps new therapists could infer how much power the family system has to resist change (and therefore how much power is needed to produce change) by being more conscious and respectful of the family's successful history of treatment failures, the chronicity of the symptom, and the seriousness of the symptom. If less experienced clinicians begin to get anxious about any of these factors, they should ask for help and seek supervision or other therapists to work with in cotherapy or on a team.

It is important during the initial phone call to find out which family members are presently in individual treatment, with whom, and for how long. A few years ago, if I learned over the phone that several of the family members were in individual treatment, I would choose not to see the family until the various individual treatments were completed. I felt that there were too many homeostats involved, stabilizing the system and making change difficult. My thinking about this issue has changed within the last few years. Now families are invited into treatment while some family members remain in individual therapy, and as the family therapy proceeds and becomes more important to the family, we are sometimes able to "peel off" the individual therapists.

The critical question here is whether the individual therapy is affecting the system and the symptom being presented to the family therapist. This question can be answered only if the family therapist sees the family. If a therapist rigidly and categorically decides not to see the family until all individual therapists are off the scene, then no determination can be made about whether these individual therapists are in the way of change in the family system.

Let me offer some examples of how individual therapy will sometimes facilitate and other times hinder marital or family therapy. If, for example, a marital therapist learns that a couple's problems escalated when one of the spouses started individual treatment, then it is evident that the individual therapy has unbalanced the couple's relationship. In such instances the marital therapist could recommend that the spouse postpone the individual work until the marital work is finished *or* encourage the spouse not in individual treatment to begin treatment. Individual treatment for the other spouse would be encouraged, not because therapy was needed, but because it would maintain some balance in the relationship. (I do something similar when one spouse is having an affair, does not want to give up either the affair or the spouse, and the monogamous spouse does not know what to do. I suggest the possibility that this spouse can have his or her own affair, which would partially rebalance the couple relationship. This suggestion is made as an intervention.)

Individual therapy may facilitate a couple's relationship if the individual therapist validates and deals with issues with one spouse that the other spouse is unwilling or unable to handle. Or, if one spouse is lonely, doesn't get enough attention from or time with the other spouse, and is unable to discuss this with his or her partner, individual therapy can provide the needed attention, time, and discussion. My sense is that it is better for the family if this spouse triangulates a therapist rather than a child.

So, the fact that some family members are in individual treatment is not automatically a contraindication to family therapy. It is incumbent on the therapist to determine the importance of the individual therapy to the individual and to the family before making unnecessary generalizations.

EVALUATING THE REFERRING CONTEXT

Further important information to be obtained during the initial phone conversation centers around the referring context. The importance of understanding the referring context cannot be overemphasized. Many times therapy cannot begin because the clinician becomes immobilized by issues stemming from the referral. Consider, for instance, the following situation:

> A family therapist once wanted to refer a family to me because the therapist was stuck after treating the family for a year or so. The wife became suicidal after her psychologist husband left her for another woman, and the family and referring therapist were worried about the wife's threats to kill herself. The

family members and the referring family therapist wanted the woman in treatment, which she refused. The referring therapist didn't know what to do, so she was making the referral to me *so I could help the family get the wife to want to attend therapy so she wouldn't kill herself.*

If I had agreed to see this woman or her family, I would have colluded even further with the family and the therapist against the wife, thereby placing the wife even further outside this collusion. Also, I would be tacitly agreeing to be responsible for keeping this woman from killing herself (see the section in Chapter 7 on suicide watch). In my mind, the family was trying to get off the hook from being responsible for a suicide, and so was the referring therapist.

I handled the situation by reminding the referring therapist that the family – not the therapist – was responsible for getting this woman into treatment. If she refused to be treated, it was the woman's and family's responsibility. I also told the referring therapist that she was the family's therapist and knew much more about the family than I did. Therefore, she should remain the therapist. If the therapist remained stuck, *after* the family got the woman into treatment, I would be happy to consult with her by watching behind the one-way mirror as a consultant or as part of a team.

This example shows how easy it is for a referral to turn into a collusion if the therapist does not think about or understand the referring context. Once the referring context is understood, one can more effectively deal with the family dynamics, as well as with the dynamics in the relationship between the referring therapist and the referred-to therapist.

Another example comes from my experience with referrals from colleagues. When I was a young and naive therapist, I did not look very carefully at the referrals I received from colleagues. After being "done in" a few times, I began to appreciate how the dynamics between the referring colleague and myself played an important role in the kinds of families which were referred and how well the treatment went. Slowly, I began to realize that referrals from colleagues fell into categories, such as "friendly," "unfriendly," "clean," and "tricky." A friendly referral, in my mind, comes from a colleague who basically respects my work or who likes me, and is making the referral because he or she is genuinely stuck, or because of some other legitimate reason, such as the patient wants to begin doing some marital or family therapy. With these friendly referrals, I do not look too closely at the referring context, because a good deal of filtering has been done already by the referring clinician. The friendly referring clinician usually calls me and explains the situation, and then I either agree or do not agree to take the referral.

The unfriendly or tricky referring context needs much closer scrutiny. If the referring therapist does not like me or respect my work, or is very competitive with me (or me with him), I have learned to direct my attention to the referring dynamics. In such cases I almost invariably contact the referring therapist before talking to the family or couple or individual and find out what is happening.

During the phone conversation with the referring therapist, I try to understand the family dynamics *and* the referring dynamics and to get a picture of the reasons for referral. Sometimes the reasons are legitimate, such as: the referring therapist is overwhelmed, the therapist needs a cotherapist or a team, or a powerful strategic approach is indicated. Other times, the reasons for referral are absolutely crazy, such as when the referring therapist wants me to deal with an unanxious piece of a system, or hold someone's hand, or keep someone from killing himself. It is interesting how full-fledged, blue-ribbon, certified systems thinkers will sometimes refer a six-year-old child to me for child therapy. When I receive such referrals, I give the referring source a consultation on how to include rather than exclude the referred person and graciously decline the referral for systemic reasons.

Sometimes I receive an ambiguous referral, which also

deserves careful scrutiny and with which I usually deal strategically. For example, a patient may call for an appointment,
and when I ask the person where she got my name, the caller
either gives the name of a therapist I have never heard of or
says she "forgot" the name of the referring person. Here, not
only did the referring therapist neglect to call, but I do not
even know his or her name. When these situations occur, I
tell the caller that I do not recognize the name of the referring
therapist and ask her to find out his name and to tell him to
call me. In these situations, I rarely receive a second call from
either the referring therapist or the prospective patient. I still
remain unsure about why I do not receive second calls from
these people, but I do know that something is up and that
the individual or family problem is not that grave. People who
want help will find out the name of the referring therapist or
referring source. People who are not willing to tell me the
name of the referring source are playing some kind of game
that I am disinterested in playing.

Another important issue to consider when talking to family member(s) during the initial phone call is whether they are
calling because they want help or because someone other than
the family wants the family to be helped. Usually during the
initial call I try to get a nonverbal (herein known as analogical) fix on the anxiety level and resistance in the system in
question. I get this fix or understanding basically from the
qualities of the voice and the description of the problem or
symptom. When my third ear tells me that there is very little
anxiety here, I inquire further about why I'm being called and
what the family wants. In these situations, I often learn that
it is not the family that is anxious, but the referring clinician.
The clinician may be more motivated for treatment than the
family!

What I do in these cases is ask the family to have the referring person call me. If the referring person calls, I then
verify my hypothesis by tracking his or her analogical responses. If the referring person is more anxious than the
referred family, I usually explain the situation to the referring
person and tell him or her that I will be quite willing to treat

the family at some later time if and when the family's anxiety level is greater. This explanation is usually sufficient and often very helpful to the referring person.

A variation of the above often occurs when an anxious member of a family calls and asks me to do family therapy with less overtly anxious members of the family. What I do in such cases is instruct the anxious family member to have the less anxious family members call me. If other members call me and indicate to me that there is sufficient anxiety in the family system, I will give the whole family an appointment.

In a similar vein, if an anxious member calls me for a family session, I will give the caller an appointment only if the whole family will come. If other family members are not willing to attend the first session, and the anxious one continues to call, I will give that person an individual appointment and try to change the system by coaching the one who comes in for treatment.

What I will *not* do is set up a *family therapy* appointment with the anxious one based only on my conversation with him or her. Often, what happens in these cases is that the family (whole or part) does not show up for treatment, or if they do come, it is a "throwaway" session, a waste of the therapist's and family's time. An enormous amount of therapeutic energy and time can be saved by dealing with these issues during the initial phone call.

Another example of looking very closely at the referring context comes from an experience I had with an analyst who called to make a referral.

> The analyst was treating a couple who came in for treatment around their son, who was chronically psychotic. However, the son refused to be treated and never came to treatment sessions; consequently, the analyst had never seen him.
>
> The analyst agreed to treat the family without the son, thinking that he could help by doing marital therapy with the couple. However, during the marital therapy the couple only talked about their son. The

anxiety in this system was escalating, and the parents were fearful that their son was going to become another Hinckley.

The analyst requested that I do family therapy while he continued to do "marital therapy." My first response to the analyst was to ask him whether he was a Democrat or a Republican. His laughter told me that he not only appreciated my sense of humor but also understood his own dilemma.

The errors made by the therapist were to agree to treat the family without seeing the son and to offer marital therapy when it was not being requested. Clearly, he did not see the collusion between the parents and the son which enabled the son to be absent from treatment sessions. The therapist was trying to stabilize a system on the family's terms rather than his own. He unwittingly helped the system to remain unchanged by agreeing with the couple's agenda to do therapy in the son's absence. The son was escalating, in part, in order to become independent and leave the family, and the therapist was treating the couple in one place, while the action was someplace else.

I explained this to the therapist, and he agreed with my assessment. I also told him to feel free to refer the family to me once the "marital work" was completed. If, in the near future, this case were referred to me, I would not begin treatment unless the son was included. I also told the therapist that the son would eventually escalate until there was enough anxiety in this system so that the couple would have no choice but to include him in treatment.

GAUGING RESISTANCE

There are many ways in which resistance can be detected during the initial phone conversation. As already mentioned, sometimes resistance is in subtle form; other times it is less than subtle.

One of my favorite expressions of resistance is an initial phone call from someone in a phone booth. Not only do I enjoy the drama, mystery, and intrigue of such a call, but I also appreciate how the caller attempts to limit the initial phone conversation to three minutes. The caller *never* has an additional nickel or dime for the additional minutes of conversation. What I do in such cases is explain to the caller that our conversation will probably take more than three minutes and that I will be happy to talk with him from a home phone. For some reason, I seldom get a second call. Now, it's possible that the caller is poor and does not have a home phone. However, I am sure a neighbor, friend, or relative does have a phone, and this phone could be used. *People with problems who want treatment do not call from phone booths* — unless they are paranoid and think their phone is tapped!

Another expression of resistance I appreciate is when the caller attempts to drag me over the coals with questions about my credentials or personal qualities. I normally respond to these questions politely, and in most cases this is sufficient. People do have a right to know a little bit about you. On the other hand, because of the referral system within which I work, people motivated for help know more about me than I do about them. Most of the referrals I get in private practice are from colleagues at the Ackerman Institute or from colleagues in private practice who do individual psychotherapy and are referring people for some systems work.

One day a caller was hauling me over the coals by questioning not only my credentials but also my age, fearing that I was too young to deal with the family problem. No longer able to restrain myself with politeness, I agreed with the woman and sent her to a colleague who was 75 years old. Two weeks later, I received a call from this same woman asking me for an appointment and complaining that my colleague was too old.

Resistance to psychotherapy can be gauged by the quality of the initial phone call as well as by some of the questions asked by the prospective patient. Sometimes this information is expressed in subtle nonverbal form; other times the resistance is blatant. The way in which the clinician deals with this resistance during the initial phone call dictates therapy outcome to some degree.

One of the things I consider while I am gathering information during the initial phone conversation is whether the family or patient is "ripe" for treatment. During this conversation I am constantly making determinations about how anxious or unhappy the caller is and whether this anxiety is greater than the resistance to change. When there is more anxiety than resistance, I will give the caller an appointment. If it is the other way around, I do not give an appointment but make a strategic explanation to the effect that the person is not yet ready for therapy or that other conditions must be met before therapy can begin. In other words, I leave the fruit on the family systems tree a bit longer, knowing that the fruit will ripen in time and the family will then be more amenable to therapy.

Here the issue of timing is crucial. There are many therapist-related issues having nothing to do with families that sometimes lead therapists to work with unripe fruit. For example, therapists just starting out in private practice are more amenable to working with unripe fruit because their needs are different from the needs of more experienced therapists. New therapists may have rescue fantasies about their patients or may be rescuing couples because they are still tuned in to their own parents' relationship. New therapists are also quite terrified of losing their first or only couple (Bergman, 1984).

> When I first started my training at the Ackerman Institute, I avoided seeing my first couple and family for the first few weeks; then I spent the rest of the year being terrified of losing these cases. After all, if I "lost" my couples, it was my fault, and more im-

portantly, if I lost my couples, how could I ever be trained?

In other words, because I was dependent upon "holding" couples because I needed them for *my* training, I lost a considerable amount, if not most, of the leverage needed to do psychotherapy, since my need for the couple was greater than their need for me. In such cases the couple is clearly in charge; when that is the case, the therapist has little clinical leverage for change.

A couple whom I treated in my first year of training returned to me about five years later. At the end of the session, the wife remarked, "You certainly have changed. I liked you a lot better when we saw you five years ago." I suspect that the wife was responding not to any great change in my personality, but to changes in my way of doing therapy. In my mind, when she encountered a therapist doing treatment, she wanted to go back five years to the frightened Dr. Homeostat oriented more toward being liked and not losing families than toward change.

Less experienced therapists may have to go through some of these experiences in order to eventually realize that they may be working with unripe fruit. One of the things I can comfortably do as an experienced family therapist is terminate treatment – even in private practice, where the consequence is always some loss of income.

The experienced therapist knows when a system is ready for change and when there is a stalemate that only the couple can break. The therapist then is at a choice point; he or she can see the couple each week until the stalemate ends or dismiss them and tell them that they should call when they are ready for change. Therapists who are not pressured by the need for patients or for income can do things like this.

Therapists who recognize and only work with ripe fruit are likely to be successful with their cases, because their control over the decision to see or not see a couple maximizes clinical leverage. In addition, these therapists probably stay alive longer as people and as therapists (see Chapter 8 on Staying Alive as a Therapist).

What about the ethical issues involved in a clinician's decision not to see a family? For me, there is no problem here, because no ethical issue is being raised. I never decide to reject a family. In most cases, families decide to reject me and/or the qualifications I make before treatment takes place.

I will never reject or refuse to see a family that meets my requirements for the first consultation. For example, if a family with a chronic, psychotic member calls me for treatment, I am always happy to set up an appointment, as long as the family agrees to come to the session with the living grandparents from *both* sides. When this condition is met, I see the family. If not, I tell the family that I will be happy to see the family when the condition is met. If the family says that the grandparents will never come, I tell the family that I cannot see them until they do. Families who refuse to act upon the therapist's conditions for treatment can and will seek treatment (or homeostasis) elsewhere.

A family is never refused treatment, although sometimes the therapist's conditions for treatment are refused by the family. My sense is that experienced family therapists set the conditions for treatment in a way which optimizes change. If the family refuses those conditions, that is the family's choice, and of course families will eventually find treatment closer to their conditions than the conditions set by an experienced therapist.

Clinicians working in agencies and clinics may have to deal with a different issue because their employer (hospital or clinic) has agreed to work with families not ready for treatment. A private, profit-making hospital may select families that are not anxious but have adequate private insurance. Or a hospital or clinic in need of census or treatment statistics might select families that are not ready so they can get the same money from the city welfare budget which they received the previous year. Hospitals might get quite upset if a clinician decides to dismiss a family from treatment if the dismissal reduces income to the hospital.

This is an old issue which still upsets my adolescent idealism; that is, public health care systems are set up backwards — with their incentive systems working in favor of "illness." If, for example, hospitals and clinics were given bonuses for effective, short-term treatment, therapy would be done differently at many of these places. Unfortunately, hospitals and clinics are usually paid not by effectiveness, but by how many patient-hours of "care" are provided. Until these incentives are reversed, clinicians working in these agencies will have to contend with families that are not ready to change.

At this point, it is perhaps useful to remind the reader of the study in which every other schizophrenic was hospitalized and the other schizophrenic was treated by a crisis intervention team on an outpatient basis (Pittman, Flomenhaft, DeYoung, Kaplan, & Langsley, 1966). The follow-up data indicated that those not hospitalized had a 50% lower recidivism rate as measured by number of days in hospital upon rehospitalization. In addition, those not hospitalized cost one-sixth the amount of money to treat compared to those hospitalized. Soon after this report was made public, Pittman was fired. It's not nice to work for a hospital and produce those kinds of results. Hospitals can't live comfortably with this kind of data, so they needed to disqualify the data, the hospital treatment, or the authors. The authors in this case were disqualified, but luckily not the data.

For those working in hospital systems, it is not news that the needs of the hospital usually take precedence over the clinical work. The end results often include enormous frustration, little therapeutic leverage, little clinical progress, and, over time, burnout in clinicians.

Although I empathize with clinicians in some agencies who must treat all families, more choices are available to these clinicians than is apparent. Many times in agencies there are many more people "requesting" treatment than there are clinicians to treat these families, and from this population therapists often have choices. In such cases, the selection of families and patients should, in part, be based upon the resistance issues discussed in this chapter. This may mean working with the most resistant, difficult families – but they also may be the most anxious and therefore the most ready to change.

I received a call from a friendly colleague of mine who was referring a family to me for various reasons: The family did not want to be treated by a female therapist or a psychiatric social worker; they *did* want to be seen by a "doctor." The referral was also being made because my colleague knew I enjoyed treating resistant families.

The moment I heard all of the therapist qualifications requested by the family, I knew there would be some "fun and games" occurring before treatment began. (By "fun and games" I am referring to the jockeying by the family and counter-jockeying by the therapist over control of the therapy which sometimes is necessary before a resistant family *begins* treatment.)

Somewhat later, I received a call from one of the family members, a young woman completing her residency in psychiatry, on my answering service. She left five different telephone and beeper numbers, since she was so busy and would be very hard to locate. I left messages at three of these numbers. One week later (the call-back time tells me that the anxiety level is low in this family), we finally connected and began the initial phone conversation.

The young resident begins by telling me that she wants family therapy for her parents and her brother, who has been a paranoid schizophrenic for the past 10 years. The brother lives with the parents, who are quite elderly, and she wants the treatment because she would like to see her brother straightened out before her parents die. (In effect, the woman does not want to take care of this brother after her parents go, so she is more anxious at this point than the brother or the parents – not a very good sign for change.) The woman then unwittingly makes a fatal mistake, telling me that she wants to make sure that, if family therapy begins, her parents are not told that she has been in individual therapy for the past two years.

I then tell the woman that there is not sufficient anxiety in this family for change to take place. I suggest that she tell her parents that she is presently in therapy, so the anxiety in her family system will increase, which is needed for successful treatment to take place. Two weeks later the woman calls, tells me she has told her parents about the individual therapy, and says she wants an appointment for the family. I then tell the woman to have her family call me for an appointment.

One week later I receive a call from the mother, who wants to know my fees. I tell her about my fees, and then she goes back to find out how much the insurance will cover. (Asking about fees and insurance is sometimes another expression of the low level of anxiety in the family.)

The family finally arrives for a consultation, and father immediately objects to the videotaping, even though I have stressed the taping to the daughter and asked her to be sure that all knew about it. Since I will not treat this family without taping, because it is so difficult, I tell the family that I cannot do the session. The family then gets into a furious fight over whether the session should begin – with father refusing to allow the taping and the rest of the family trying to coax him into signing the release. I have already told the family that the interview cannot begin without all their signatures on the consent form. The fight within the family ends when the daughter, infuriated with the father, runs hysterically out of the room. The family then pays the fee for a two-hour consultation and leaves.

The next day mother calls, suggesting that my fee was too high, since the family was not seen. I explain to the mother that the space was reserved for them and it was my time that they were paying for. Daughter then calls a week later to apologize for the fight and for her rude behavior.

The brother then calls me about two weeks later and asks whether I will reconsider doing the session without tape. Although sympathetic with the brother, I refuse to see this family without taping. (I was convinced that this would be a tough family to change, and if I was not working with a team or cotherapist, I at least needed the tape to show a colleague of mine, in the likely instance of my getting stuck with this family.) *Families who want help will not fuss over the videotaping, since the tape is used only for professional and consulting purposes.*

My guess is that I'll be getting a call from this family when they are ready to change.

For one entire year of the eight years I worked with a strategic team treating only "resistant" families, we practiced "losing" families. When there was doubt about whether a family should be seen, we would often not see the family, instead giving them a strategic message. The more we practiced not seeing families, the more power or therapeutic leverage we obtained. In most cases, after we refused to see the family, they became more amenable to treatment. I think the clinician's fear of losing families keeps a system from changing and keeps the therapist from having therapeutic leverage. By fearing the loss of a family, and therefore having little clinical leverage, the clinician unwittingly winds up babysitting rather than doing treatment. Only when the family needs the therapist more than the therapist needs the family is change optimal.

A couple came to us to try to change their 30-year-old chronically psychotic son, who had been in and out of hospitals and individual therapy for the past 11 years. The boy hung around the house dressed in

rags and perferred sleeping in the family's garage to
his own room. We turned the family down for treatment and at the end of the consultation we gave the
family the following message:

*It is clear to the team from the information gath-
ered in this consultation that Matthew (the psychotic
son) is basically an 80-year-old grandfather trapped
in the body of a 30-year-old. Not only does Matthew
emotionally function as the father his parents miss
the most, but he also acts and looks like an 80-year-
old middle-class retiree. His income is based upon
Social Security (SSI) and money from his children
(parents); he migrates like a retired snowbird, who
goes south after the High Holy Days, and returns to
New York around Passover. His needs for food, shel-
ter, and clothing are modest, and his eccentricity and
incipient senility are commensurate with his age.*

*Mother and father become upset and frustrated
when they try to get Matthew to act like a 30-year-
old without realizing and appreciating that they both
need this beloved 80-year-old father. Clearly, mother
and father must learn to appreciate, love, and respect
Matthew as their father rather than trying to change
his behaviors.*

*Therefore, we feel that mother and father should
cease trying to change Matthew, and enjoy, honor,
and respect their beloved 80-year-old-father. When
mother and father try to annually change Matthew
during the holidays, we recommend that the family
call Dr. Bergman, who will be happy to help mother
and father mourn the loss of their 30-year-old son, and
also help them to learn to enjoy more of their 80-year-
old father.*

Sincerely,
The Brief Therapy Team

This is the letter which we gave to the family and sent to Matthew (since he never attended the session). There was no need to see this family, since there was little anxiety in the system. Therefore, we declined to see the family, leaving them instead with a strategic message.

I suspect that the letter increased the tension in the family and perhaps mobilized Matthew to change. If Matthew did not change and the system steamed up again, I'm sure the parents knew that we would not see them until there was much more steam in this system or until they were really fed up with their 30-year-old Baby Huey and "really" ready to help this kid grow up.

It would be helpful and instructive if hospitals and clinics gave all therapists a one-year practicum sabbatical which permitted them to lose families. Only then could beginning clinicians begin appreciating how powerful they and the therapy could be when they strategically chose to lose families.

Which family members are invited to the first session

One of the most confusing issues I experienced during my family therapy training was the question of which family members are invited to the first session. In my mind, Carl Whitaker was saying that you needed three generations, Jay Haley was talking about the whole household, and Murray Bowen was suggesting bringing in the most powerful or motivated person in the family. What I have come to realize, after several years of clinical work, is that all three were right. There are complicated issues involved in the selection of families and in "inviting" resistant families into treatment.

After the clinical information has been obtained from the initial telephone call and the pretreatment jockeying for position has been completed, the next important step in treating resistant families is deciding which family members are to be invited to the first session. This is a point where important choices are made. Who gets invited, the family's reaction to the invitation, and the clinician's reaction to the family will in part determine whether treatment begins and how successful the treatment will be.

With serious symptoms such as psychosis, anorexia, or suicidal depression, or with a chronic history of a symptom, I will not see a family unless all people in the household are willing to attend the first session. This is clearly a choice point for clinicians; some therapists might be willing to work with less than a "full deck of cards" (all people living in one household). However, when a family has a serious or chronic symptom, working with less than the entire household of members gives the clinician much less leverage, flexibility, and information to help the family change.

When the clinician chooses to work with less than the full household of family members, there is invariably less therapeutic leverage, because the therapist is being permitted to see only that part of a family system which the family decides to show. For example, when one or several of the children in a household "refuse" to show up for the first session, these family members are colluding with the parents or grandparents and are receiving signals not to attend therapy. When the clinician agrees to see only part of the household, he or she is then colluding with the collusion within the family. Therapists are then playing with less than a full deck of cards. *Families who want treatment will get all members of the family into the first session.* Families who cannot or will not do so need more time to ripen before they are ready for treatment.

Working with less than a full household of members also reduces therapeutic flexibility, as well as the clinical leverage needed to change difficult families. The more family members there are in a room, the more information one gathers about how the family system operates. In addition, with a full household present, many more choices and possible interventions, rituals, and interpretations can be made.

In summary, when working with a resistant family with serious or chronic symptoms, the probability of effecting change without seeing the entire household for the initial interview is minimal. Seeing less than the whole household results in a collusion between the therapist and the family, which results in the therapist's *stabilizing* rather than changing the family. One must remember that refusing to see less than a full household always leaves the family the choice of seeing a therapist who will agree with the family's agenda to work with fewer members. Families sometimes go "shopping" for the therapist who will go along with them. What is important is that the serious clinician, who is interested in *changing* rather than stabilizing the situation, does not ethically or clinically have to go along with the family's agenda.

A complicated situation occurs when the identified patient is in his or her twenties or thirties and is living at home with the parents. Other siblings may be living in their own households. When the nonsymptomatic sibs are living within traveling distance, the first session should include them as well. When there are many siblings, and these sibs are scattered all over the country, I usually insist that the first session include the parents, the identified patient, and at least one other "nonsymptomatic" sib. The more nonsymptomatic sibs able to attend, the more information and therapeutic leverage in the session.

There are many reasons for insisting upon the inclusion of at least one nonsymptomatic sib. Often one finds a situation where a chronic symptom is shown by the last bird in the nest, and the parents have been heroically struggling for the past 15 years to "help" this "last bird" grow up and leave the nest. The 15-year history of the family's efforts also includes a detailed account of the family's successfully defeating many mental health professionals. When one interviews this threesome, their explanations, tears, statements, and responses to one another have the quality of an old play, being performed for the 500th time. This triangle appears "frozen," standard, and pat. The chances of getting into this family and finding crucial information necessary to change the system are minimal. The inclusion of another sibling somewhat changes this frozen system in the treatment room, throws the play off, and gives the clinician more opportunities to get into the family, obtain information, and change the system with interventions which *include* this nonsymptomatic sibling. (One can almost "see" the anxiety level increase when inclusion of the nonsymptomatic sib is suggested. This increased anxiety further supports the notion that this sibling is needed for change to take place in such frozen families.)

Just as the remaining triangle (mother, father, IP) has become more and more frozen as each of the other older children has left the household, this triangle becomes more and more thawed out with the inclusion of additional sibs in the initial treatment session. The greater the number of additional sibs, the more fluid this remaining frozen triangle will be, and hence, the more opportunities for therapeutic change. Thus, when working with a chronic system with two or more siblings, the inclusion of a nonsymptomatic sib is a prerequisite for the first treatment session.

The sibling relationship is especially important when there are only two siblings – one the IP, and the other living very far away from the parents, married, with children, and successful. Here it seems as if there is one scapegoat and one grace-child. And often there is a metaphorical complementarity between the "symptoms" of the two children such as when one sibling is a certified psychotic and the other a certified psychiatrist, psychologist, or social worker.

With such families, the treatment initially begins with the frozen triangle, with the hope and expectation that the other sibling will eventually be brought into treatment for at least one consultation. When this nonsymptomatic sib does eventually come in, the system appears to shift immediately. Usually some prescription is then made which includes this nonsymptomatic sibling. One of the main advantages of having this sib in the session is that the therapist can put the IP and the non-IP sib on the same level. Usually the prescription made to the family shows how each child, in his or her own way, is protecting the parents.

Experience also suggests that this nonsymptomatic sib usually will not or cannot be seen at the initial treatment session. The family makes up all kinds of excuses for the exclusion of this person. However, after the treatment begins and the therapist has joined the family, the chances of getting the family to bring in this sib for a consultation improve considerably. I might also add that never being able to see this sib, or this family with this sib, minimizes the opportunities to thaw out this system and therefore bring about change.

PRE-FIRST-SESSION MANEUVERS

Once the initial phone call has been completed, and the conditions have been set as to which family members will come to the first session, the pretreatment maneuvers are far from over with some resistant families. Some families are very enterprising and have a wealth of ways to block arriving for the first session.

A very chaotic family, consisting of a manic-depressive mother, her 10-year-old son who was recently kicked out of a residental placement center for being "impossible," and the mother's parents, were interviewed by a senior, experienced colleague of mine. The family defeated the colleague in less than 40 minutes, and the colleague referred the family to me because he knew I liked this kind of challenge.

An appointment was made with this family. Then, about three hours before the first session was to take place, I received a telephone call from the mother. Over the phone, mother told me that she and her parents wanted to attend the first session, but the boy refused to come in. She wanted to know what to do. I then told the mother that she should pick him up and get him to the session. Mother then told me that the "boy" weighs 225 pounds, and that she can't pick him up. I then told the mother to rent an ambulance with two burly attendants and get the boy to the session. Mother then asked me whether this was a standard procedure at the Institute with these cases, and I said, "yes." Mother then asked if Medicaid would pick up the tab on the ambulance and the

burly attendants. I told her I didn't know. The family
arrived on time for the initial session and came by
subway.

In this situation, I out-blocked the family. I stayed with
the "logic" of the reason why the family was unable to attend,
pushing this logic until my logic was more powerful than the
logic in the initial block. At one level, this family wanted to
attend therapy; they were also at the same time afraid of
change. Once the block against the resistance to treatment
was made, the family was able to come in.

Another presession resistance maneuver which I often experience centers around the time and date of the first session.
An appointment is offered to a family, and they can't make
it. Another appointment date is impossible for them. It's absolutely amazing how a family can be living in an impossible, crazy household, call for an appointment, and then be
unable to make the first appointment because of a prior bowl-
ing date, card game, etc. After two possible appointments are
refused by the family, they are told that the next possible appointment will be two or three months later. In most cases,
the family then takes the appointment date which was orig-
inally offered.

Another variation of this occurs when the family agrees
to the first appointment but does not show up. Instead they
call, usually less than an hour before the appointment, and
give some excuse for not being able to attend. The proximity
of the cancellation to the appointment time tells the clinician
that this is resistance to treatment rather than a genuine
scheduling issue. When the family asks for another appointment, I give them a date one month later. If this second appointment is canceled, I might give them the next appointment two months later.

One of the families we were treating, who canceled several
times, accused us of punishing them with longer intervals of
time between sessions because of frequent cancellation of appointments made by the family. We then told this family that
this was not the case and that our scheduling determined the

time intervals between sessions. Normally, families who often cancel will determine the time interval between sessions, since they know best how to calibrate the rate and amount of change the family system can tolerate. This avoids any potential power struggle between the clinician and the family. Clinicians should be respectful of the fact that the family will determine the intersession interval (if they cancel often) and that this is the family's message to the therapist about how fast (or slow) treatment should move.

SUMMARY

This chapter has touched on some of the issues involved in recognizing and selecting resistant families for treatment. There are an infinite number of ways in which these families will resist treatment, and just as many ways in which the clinician can deal with this resistance. It is important that the clinician distinguish between what is and is not resistance and act accordingly. Only when these distinctions are comfortably made and considered by the clinician can the effective treatment of these resistant families begin.

2

CAPTURING FAMILIES

This chapter will address some of the issues involved in the complicated process of capturing resistant families. Some of these issues are clear in my mind and relatively easy to elucidate. However, there are other issues which seem ambiguous, fuzzy, and analogical in nature; therefore, at times linear, rational explanations can only approximate what I am trying to describe.

When a family, resistant or not, comes in for treatment, a relationship begins to form between the therapist and the family. How that relationship develops depends in part on what the therapist does and on what the family shows. Here the word "show" is taken from the Milan Group's work, where a distinction is made between what *is* and what is *shown* (Palazzoli, Boscolo, Cecchin, & Prata, 1978). The Milan Group implies that often what a family shows is a maneuver or an overt posture—not necessarily what the family *is* or what the family is *really* feeling or thinking. Thinking in terms of "show" assists the clinician in remaining meta to a family system, which invariably gives the therapist more understanding and control over the treatment.

Now, there are many possible therapeutic postures; which ones are chosen by the therapist will in part influence how the relationship between the therapist and the family is initially defined and develops over time. In addition, part of the process of defining the relationship between therapist and family involves engaging the family in treatment. Here, too, the clinician has many choices. Some of these possible choices are discussed in greater detail below.

JOINING WHILE REMAINING META TO THE SYSTEM

When I begin working with a resistant family, I actively join with the family in as many ways as possible. Here, I use "join" very much the way Minuchin (1974) uses the term in his work. That is, I look for opportunities to connect with the family. In my mind, the more I join and connect with the family, and the more connected the family experiences me, the more leverage I will have to help the family change. This is also similar to Milton Erickson's way of working (Haley, 1967). On the other hand, the less connected I feel towards the family, and they towards me, the less leverage I will have.

When I am conducting the initial interview, I attempt to join with the family in as many ways as possible. I will underscore any similarities between me and the family as the family unfolds its unique history. These similarities might involve common histories (for example, being born and raised in Brooklyn and being of similar socioeconomic background), similar family structure (for example, having the same birth order), cultural similarities, interests, and enthusiasms. In addition, I will take as many opportunities to join affectively with family members by disclosing similarities in areas which have a high degree of emotionality — for example, if a family member has a bizarre sense of humor similar to mine, or is a jazz musician, or loves to cook and eat foods. In addition, there are nonverbal expressions of joining; for example, I may nonverbally signal to someone in the family that I really understand what he is struggling with or saying.

While joining with a family is necessary, it is not sufficient. Joining must be combined with strategies for changing families, particularly when working with resistant families. Therapists must learn to join and connect with the family and yet, at the same time, stay emotionally uninvolved, in a meta position. They should not become entangled in the family's emotionality. This may appear to be contradictory, but it is not. One can learn to stay emotionally connected to the family and at the same time maintain a distance that keeps the therapist out of the powerful family emotional system with its potential to engulf or immobilize him.

There are many ways of remaining meta to a family system. One way is to see the provocative things a family presents to a therapist as maneuvers — such as homicide-, suicide-, matricide-, or castration-maneuvers (Palazzoli et al., 1978). When these events are seen as maneuvers by the therapist, it is less likely that the therapist will be upset and fooled by them; consequently, the therapist will be able to understand the family system on his terms rather than on the family's terms. Thus one way to stay meta is to see provocative, emotional maneuvers as just that and not "the real thing."

A maneuver typical of families of schizophrenics is the "Doctor, we won't be able to do this without you" ploy. In such cases, the therapist has previously instructed the parents that they should agree upon the next step for their son or daughter and be able to act upon this agreement. In many cases, the next step is for their grown child to move out of the house, as he should have done years earlier. As soon as the parents agree that it would be best for the son to live on his own, the son escalates and tries to get back into the house by various means. The therapist must avoid being seduced into playing the ensuing game.

> One of my patients, told it was time to find his own apartment, "showed" psychosis, brain damage, and unkempt, disheveled, bowery-type behavior; he started to go to the parents' friends for handouts, food, clothes, etc.
>
> The parents called me daily in a panic, asking for help. Was he brain damaged? Was he going to commit murder? Was it safe for him to roam the community? My instructions to the parents remained the same, as I stayed meta to the system; that is, I told them to maintain their agreement and do whatever

they agreed to do until their son stopped acting this way. The other thing they could do, of course, was to take the boy back into the house, which was the secret agenda of one of the parents.

The more the parents went helpless as their son escalated, the more they called me with requests for instructions. Now, the parents knew what to do, but emotionally they were having a hard time because: 1) they had never set boundaries or limits for this child; and 2) if they truly got together and set boundaries and consequences, the son would grow up and leave—leaving the couple alone for the first time in 30 years. Hence, they had a big investment in not agreeing on parenting and in keeping their overgrown last bird in their nest.

While understanding how hard this was for the parents, I had to stay out of the emotionality of the family situation because: 1) it was my instruction that they could now do whatever they pleased with their son as long as they were in agreement; and 2) the longer the parents could keep the son out of the house, and the son could stay out of the house, the easier it would be for the son to grow up, and the parents to move to the next stage in their own development.

Another way of remaining meta to a family system is to have a life philosophy of not taking too many things seriously. When therapists get caught up in the deadly seriousness and earnestness of the family's presenting problems, they lose their meta positions and therefore their effectiveness as therapists. Additional ways of remaining meta to a system are related to issues of staying alive as a therapist (see Chapter 8).

CAPTURING BY JUJITSU

I was giving a workshop on brief therapy with resistant families; during one break a conferee came up to me and pointed out that she thought I "seduced" difficult families into treatment. She was commenting on this after I had shown an edited videotape of a family which was very fused, intense, attacking, blaming, violent, and basically "terrible," both to each other and to the therapist. The conferee went on to point out that the "seduction" consisted of my remaining in the room with the family, despite all this terrifying stuff, showing a tranquil, "Would you mind passing the toast, please?" quality towards the family.

Although I do not think the term "seduction" is accurate, this conferee did have a point. I feel more comfortable using the term *jujitsu* to describe my response to a family's terrifying maneuvers. This term has also been used by my favorite therapist, Carl Whitaker, who describes how good students of psychotherapy proceed over time up the martial arts ladder from judo to jujitsu to akedo (Whitaker, 1972).

Jujitsu is a martial art where one uses the strengths and weight of an adversary to disable him. It takes about 20 years to master both physically and mentally. In therapy, it is an attempt on the therapist's part to take advantage of a high anxiety situation by reducing somewhat the ambivalence towards treatment and lowering the family's resistance. Jujitsu is a posture: The family's resistance towards treatment pushes against the therapist, and the therapist ducks or passively moves sideways, resulting in the family's push against treatment propelling them into the arms of the therapist. Although I have never formerly studied this martial art, and although I was raised in Brooklyn rather than in Tokyo, I think I served an 18-year apprenticeship in jujitsu in my family of origin.

I come from a very fused, noisy family, where what is said is not meant and what is felt and experienced is often not overtly expressed. Instead, family members' insides, as well as the definition of relationships between people in this family, are camouflaged by yelling, blaming, attacking, and loudness. Engineers would describe this system as having enormous noise and very little signal.

As a consequence of this apprenticeship, I learned very early in life to listen to the music rather than the lyrics of any ongoing family opera and particularly to pay attention *only* to the music when there is a contradiction between the music and the lyrics. In other words, in my mind, if the analogics (nonverbals) do not fit with the words (verbals), I normally disregarded the overt communication *content* of what is being said. I stop thinking with my left hemisphere and put my right hemisphere on automatic pilot (its usual mode anyway).

Therefore, to do family therapy with terrifying, crazy families is like a homecoming for me. I basically stay in the room, turn my left hemisphere off, relax, see most of what is being said as noise, a show, a display, and wait until the overture to this black musical comedy is over. There may even be an affectionate smile in my eyes, which is communicated to the family. Usually the family induces in me some warm, affectionate, nostalgic feeling, similar to the misty feelings aroused in others by the the smell of fresh baked bread or chicken soup.

My initial warm, affectionate response to the maneuvers of chaotic, terrifying families probably confuses the hell out of them. More importantly, my response tells them that their display will not work (in fact, I secretly giggle inside) and that I know what they are doing. The latter, at some level, may be comforting to the family, because they know that I know; this might engender relief, security, and confidence in me or the therapy or both.

These fused families are also very insecure, and some of their insecurity comes out in the form of competitiveness. Now, often by the time these families are referred to me, they have already outwitted and outclassed many other therapists, whom they probably contemptuously place in the bush-leagues compared to themselves. When the family members do not knock me over with their antics, which have successfully killed other therapists, the family's competitiveness is probably activated; also, there is probably some secret excitement about this new worthy opponent. Their excitement that they have worked their way up from the minor leagues and are now playing hardball in a major league further connects the family to me and to the treatment. There is always some respect among thieves.

CAPTURING WITH REFRAMING, INTRIGUE, AND MYSTERY

The technique of reframing has been around a long time in the field of psychotherapy. Different theories of therapy have different terms to describe this phenomenon. In psychoanalysis, some reframings are called interpretations; the Milan Group (Palazzoli et al., 1978) refers to this process as "positive connotation"; and the term "reframing" itself comes from the work of the Palo Alto group (Watzlawick, Weakland, & Fisch, 1974).

Reframing occurs most often in psychotherapy when a therapist offers a new way of looking at something – a way that is different from the way in which the patient has perceived the same phenomenon. If the reframing is presented to the patient in a way which is consistent with the way he thinks, organizes his life or perceives his world, the reframing is more likely to be accepted. Here, the reframing is made in a way which is consistent with the patient's language, a process which was artfully illustrated in Milton Erickson's work (Haley, 1967).

Reframing in itself has enormous therapeutic power. Patients react to an effective reframing with responses such as surprise, startle, and sometimes, excitement. When a reframing is accepted, not only the perception but also the affect associated with the perception change. Patients seem to become unstuck from their old position in their lives or in their families. And often, one finds that changes in behavior follow this change in perception. So the therapeutic implications of reframing are quite powerful – independent of the theory of therapy in which the reframing is used.

A few examples will suffice. One of the most powerful and general reframings I use is when I elaborate to a family how a child's symptom protects the family, and how it particularly protects the parents or the marital couple by bringing the couple together and/or deflecting the couple's attention away from the marriage or the couple's parents. When parents come into treatment with a kid whom they see as "mad" or "bad," the last perception or explanation they expect from a therapist is that the symptomatic child is protecting them. Once they even consider the reframing as a possible explanation, the system begins to change.

Reframing often works effectively when a couple comes in for treatment and the marital conflict is contained by one partner's taking full responsibility for the problems in the marriage. This is often the case, for example, when the presenting problem is drug or alcohol abuse in one partner, with the other partner either blaming or feeling victimized by the problem. Often, I tell the couple that the abuser is absorbing tension in the marriage for both partners and that the non-drug-abusing partner should appreciate and thank the abuser for absorbing the tension for both rather than just for him- or herself. At the end of such sessions, I give the couple a ritual in which I tell the abuser that he must continue to absorb tension for the couple. I also tell the non-abuser that when she starts getting anxious she should offer her husband a drink, or pot, or some cocaine, or whatever the abuse appears to be (see "Have another drink, dear!" in Chapter 6). Two weeks following this assignment (which is the usual intersession interval I use with couples), the spouses come in with the marital conflict overt and no longer lodged in the symptom; they may be fighting or one partner may be threatening to end the marriage. When this happens the focus shifts from the abuse to the conflicts in the couple's relationship. Once the marital conflict is overt and the couple is motivated to work on the relationship, the clinician is no longer trapped by having to deal with the substance abuse as the *only* problem.

Another common reframing demonstates to a couple how their marital fights protect the relationships each of the partners has with his or her parents. I then continue the treatment by prescribing rituals the partners are to do with each other, as well as rituals they are to do with their parents. Couples are quite surprised and intrigued to learn how their fights are connected to their "marriages" with their parents.

A young couple came in for treatment because of tremendous fighting in the relationship. They had lived together for the past seven years, but had been married for less than six months. The overt fighting was around two out of the three classical control issues in marriages: money and sex. (The relationship was too new for them to fight over the third issue, namely kids.)

During the initial interview, it became evident that one of the reasons the partners were having such a hard time was that the wife was still married to her maternal grandmother and the husband to his mother.

We gave the couple the following ritual: On odd days, the husband was to be in charge of sex, and to have as much as he wished, with the wife acting graciously; on even days of the week, the wife was in charge of spending money, and husband was to follow graciously; on Sunday, the spouses were to find a new and more creative way of trying to control each other. (One of the lighter and funnier parts of this work is watching the reactions when you prescribe as homework what people claim they want. When husband heard that he could have as much sex as he wanted on odd days, he gasped and became quite anxious.)

Now where do wife's grandmother and husband's mother fit in here? From the emotional reactions of the partners when they were decribing their relationships with their families of origin, it was clear that neither would "buy" that they were still married to somebody else. In addition, we also were not very confident that the couple would do the homework. So we brought wife's grandmother and husband's mother in indirectly, metaphorically, and as a penalty, by telling the husband that if he didn't do the homework, he would have to call his mother and ask her for advice. The wife would have to do the same with her grandmother if she did not do her homework. Here the reframing of each partner's being married to some-

one in the family of origin was implicit in the ritual.
The couple did the homework, and as a consequence,
the focus of the therapy shifted away from the power
struggle. If the partners were not connected to individuals in their families of origin in this way, we would
not have used this particular "penalty."

Let me emphasize that when I use reframings I am not
making up something out of thin air. When I tell a couple that
a drug abuser is absorbing tension for the couple, *I believe*
this to be the case. The same thing is true when I tell parents
how a child's symptom protects them or when I tell spouses
how a marital fight might protect one partner's relationship
with his parents or, in the above case, with a grandparent. If
and when the reframing is not systemically "true," it will probably have less therapeutic power. The reframing becomes an
opportunity to share with a family a powerful alternative explanation of an inexplicable, painful situation.

Using reframing to capture families has not been given
much attention in the literature. When a patient or family responds favorably to a reframing, there is movement towards
the therapist or therapy. It is as if a patient or family has
been struggling for years to figure out a puzzle. Suddenly,
the therapist has offered an answer or solution to this puzzle, and the patient or family is grateful and sometimes excited about having more knowledge about this life puzzle. As
a consequence, the family members are more in charge of
their lives. The excitement and gratitude move patients closer
to the therapist—hence, one of the capturing qualities of using reframing in treatment.

When the reframing is positive, the therapeutic power and
capturing quality of the reframing are increased. For some
reason, the exploration of which goes beyond the scope of this
book, people are inclined to perceive and explain their psychological worlds in negative ways. In addition, there is a
tendency for people to explain their behaviors and those of
others in linear, causal, and sometimes blaming ways. It is
as if people "naturally" explain their worlds by looking at the

"underside" or negative side of a circular relationship, rather than the "up" or positive side.

When a positive connotation is used, not only is it powerful and capturing because of its "positivity," but it also informs the patient with systems information about the other side of a cycle. When this happens, some formerly painful, stuck perception or position becomes less mysterious for a patient or family. Thus, the capturing qualities of a reframing—both because it brings new clarity and because it offers a different, positive point of view—cannot be overemphasized.

Reframing a symptom as protective of other people in the family is positive. Prior to the reframing a family may have seen the patient as bad, mad, mean, or spoiled. Reframing a husband's impotence as protective of his wife's anxiety about her frigidity is positive, at least for the husband, and shifts the focus in the family. Sometimes a shift in focus as to who is responsible for the problem is sufficient to change a symptom and system.

I might just note that although therapists use positive connotation in their interpretations, there is always an implied negative connotation for a different individual in the family system. A child's protection of a parent is positive, and a parent's need for protection is negative. The parent who is being "protected" by the child's symptom may and often will object to this interpretation. One of the ways in which the therapist gets around this objection is say that it is the *child's perception* that the parent needs to be protected or that the marriage will be endangered if the child's symptom disappears. In such cases the "reality" of the situation is less important than the parents' need to *change the child's perception of his or her need to protect.* In most cases, the *only* way the parents can change the child's perception is to change the marriage or make some other important systems shift.

Everyone knows about the capturing qualities inherent in intrigue. Witness people's reactions when a storyteller forgets the punchline or the end of a story. Or witness what goes on when someone patiently listens to a person who stutters. In both cases, the listeners are being captured or captivated by the speaker. In addition, in both cases the listener's frustration is a consequence of being intrigued and then let down. The captivating qualities of intrigue and mystery are all too evident when watching a good Hitchcock film. The filmmaker was a genius in his understanding and use of intrigue, mystery, and suspense in capturing audiences.

Although no one expects a therapist to make use of intrigue to capture families in the way that Hitchcock captured audiences, some paradoxical and strategic interventions are so captivating that they can be used to lure the family into change.

A family was referred to me because of the impossible behaviors of the 10-year-old son, whose first name was Fido. (The name has been changed for purposes of confidentiality, but the reader should know that the boy's real name was also a classical dog's name.) Fido hung out of windows from the 40th floor of his apartment building whenever he didn't get his way. In addition, he wrote offensive graffiti in his room, in the apartment elevator, and on buildings near his apartment. Fido also got into fights, night and day, with his mother and new stepfather. He also fought with his father, who had been divorced by his mother five years earlier.

The first treatment session included Fido, his older brother, his mother, and his stepfather, all of whom lived in the same apartment. Also included in this session were Fido's father and his girlfriend, who lived in a different apartment nearby. Fido spent part of the week in father's apartment and the remainder of the week with his mother and stepfather.

After the first session it became clear that Fido's behavior protected one of three couples: the recent marriage of his mother and stepfather; the old marriage and unresolved divorce of his mother and father; or the potential new relationship of his father and

father's girlfriend, which appeared quite fragile. What
was unclear in the therapist's mind was which marriage Fido was protecting, since it could have been
any one of the three. The following prescription from
a team was given to this family after the third session.

*We believe that Fido protects all three couples —
girlfriend and father; father and mother; and mother
and new stepfather — by acting the way he does. If
Fido stopped being a watchdog, he would force the
issue of whether stepfather and mother are married,
whether girlfriend and father will be married, and
whether father and mother can say goodbye. Because
Fido feels that any one of these decisions might endanger a beloved parent, he allows his parents only
to be married to him. For the following month, all
three couples must watch their own backyards very
closely to determine which backyard their beloved
watchdog is guarding.*

In this prescription to the family, the mystery and
intrigue were evident, and the family was somewhat
captivated by the message, which had a latent irre-
sistibility about it. Fido's obnoxious behavior was reframed into wisdom; he knew something that the
family did not know. The three family couples were
told that they must focus on the symptoms even
more than they were already doing, because within
those symptoms was metaphorically hidden something about *their own lives* rather than Fido's problems.

Soon after, father broke up with his girlfriend, and
mother and stepfather were able to set up boundaries
which Fido could respect. Father's fury towards mother, acted out through Fido, was redirected towards
the therapist in the form of nonpayment. Three years
later, father has not yet paid his share of the treat-

ment bill, but Fido is doing well in school and no
longer having behavioral problems.

The prescription is reminiscent of Agatha Christie's *Murder
on the Orient Express*, where someone is murdered and all
of the passengers on the train are suspects. Only two people
know who the murderer is – the murderer and eventually the
inspector who solves the case. There is enormous intrigue until the case is solved. Such intrigue and mystery are experienced by the family as a consequence of the intervention,
since the only people who know what's going on are perhaps
Fido and eventually the therapist. Families will move towards treatment when intrigue is used in the same way that
readers or moviegoers move towards a good mystery or sus-
penseful film.

CAPTURE BY THE DANCE OF THE SEVEN VEILS

Many times, when resistant families seek treatment, there
is considerable ambivalence about whether they will commit
themselves to family therapy. On the one hand, families are
seeking treatment because of the anxiety and pain they are
currently experiencing. On the other hand, treatment is
feared because of the family's perception of the possible consequences of change. Often, families fear that the consequences of treatment will lead to a family member's leaving
(and this fear is justified).

Leaving can take many forms: A child grows up and leaves
in the normal course of events; or one partner is prompted
to leave the marriage after the last child leaves; or a grandparent dies and upsets a delicate marital balance. Fear of leaving may take many forms, such as becoming ill, depressed,
or psychotic. Thus, although resistant families often call for
help, they usually attend the first session with strongly ambivalent feelings about change. When these ambivalent feelings are sensed by the therapist in the first session, one of
the first goals of treatment is to intervene in a way that increases commitment to the family treatment. Dealing direct-

ly with the presenting symptom cannot begin until the family's resistance to the treatment has been reduced. In such cases, one way in which resistance can be reduced is with the use of a posture that I call the "dance of the seven veils."

This dance involves the therapist's taking a posture symmetrical to the family's ambivalent posture. When the family in essence declares, "We want help, but don't want you to change us," my response is, "I would love to help you, but am not sure I can." This posture is reflected in the first prescription to the family, which is directed not only to the symptom, but also to the commitment to the treatment. A few examples of this posture from actual cases will suffice. In these cases, the family's ambivalence towards treatment is mirrored by the therapist's ambivalence towards helping, using a split message from the team (behind a one-way screen) and from the therapist.

After an initial session, the team delivered this report:

> *There is no question that family therapy can help this family deal with the problems discussed in this first session. The team, however, feels from the information gathered during this consultation that if family therapy were to help the parents work together effectively to deal with the children's problems, this would put a strain on mother's relationship with her parents.*
>
> *The team feels that the children, sensing how difficult this would be for the parents, will by their behaviors dictate whether a second consultation will take place. The next consultation will be scheduled on Dec. 12 at 10 a.m.*
>
> *The Brief Therapy Team*

This was a family where the parents put themselves in a victim, helpless, and child-like position, and where the parents' dynamics and needs were played out by the children and

the children's symptoms. The family came in for treatment
because two of the four children had been hospitalized for depression and psychotic episodes.

This team message was given to this family because their
ambivalence towards treatment was analogically displayed
throughout the first session. The ambivalence was displayed
in the form of the parents' not showing enough anxiety about
their two symptomatic children. After working with such
families over the years, experienced clinicians know when a
family is and is not anxious about the presenting symptoms.
When the clinician sees little anxiety, there is also little leverage for change. Several parts of the message are addressed
to the ambivalence, and these parts make up some of the
steps involved in the "dance of the seven veils."

The ambivalent splits by the family towards the treatment
are mirrored by the therapeutic splits expressed in the message. The first split is between the therapists and the team.
The split comes out of the therapists' analogically indicating
that they want to help the family, while the team is doubt-
ful and pessimistic. A second split is saying that the parents
say they want treatment, but the children probably will not
cooperate. The third split is saying that the family, on the
one hand, wants treatment, but the family's loyalty (particularly mother's loyalty to her mother) would be in jeopardy if
the treatment were successful.

The ambivalent splits in the therapeutic message attempt
to counter the family's ambivalent splits towards the treatment. This consequently reduces resistance to the treatment
and moves the family toward rather than away from therapy.
In addition, the message prescribes the resistance by telling
the children that they must act out the family's resistance,
as they already do.

Finally, the message implies that the children will make
the decision about whether the therapy should begin. This
prescription moves the family toward the therapeutic goal of
getting the parents back in charge of the family. The message
implies that the children will decide for the parents, which
is an attempt on the therapists' part to mobilize the parents
to begin taking charge and acting like parents.

Part of the above message is often used in treatment with families who are ambivalent about beginning treatment, that is, the labeling of the first session as *not* a session. When resistance is high about therapy, the first session is labeled a consultation, conversation, family gathering, or chat—namely, anything but therapy. Labeling these initial sessions is part of the dance, until a contract (implied or agreed) is reached by the family and the therapist.

Quite often, two or three initial consultations or family "conversations" are needed before the resistance is sufficiently reduced. Then, the therapist asks the family members what they want from treatment and reaches some form of contractual agreement with them. Many times families ask during the second "conversation" whether the treatment has begun. Treatment, of course, begins when the first contact is made with the family, but this is not overtly acknowledged until a contract is made or resistance is reduced. The fact that a family asks whether treatment has begun suggests that not calling the initial sessions treatment is an effective way of reducing resistance.

Another example of the dance of the seven veils was used at the end of an initial consultation with a family who asked for help with their 30-year-old daughter, Marion, who had been psychotic and in and out of hospitals for the past eight years. Two of the three other living children in this family had moved far from the parental home, and another child, age 25, was killed in an auto accident (which appeared to the therapists to have been a suicide). Mother's father and brother had committed suicide, and father's only brother died of pneumonia at age 15.

Marion and the two parents remained at home, locked in a frozen triangle (see Chapter 1). During the first session, it appeared that Marion's psychotic behavior was the underbelly of her parents' feelings and experiences. Marion was the emotional one, whereas the parents appeared to be rigid, overintellectualized, and brittle. The unspoken family fear was that if Marion became normal, there would no longer be someone in the family to experience and act out the parents' unexpressed underbelly. The following prescription was given to the family from the team at the end of the first session:

> *This is a caring and courageous family which has survived major losses. Of the children, Marion has been extremely sensitive, acutely experiencing everything that the family has gone through. In one way, her sensitivity has led Marion to be an artist; in another way, her sensitivity has produced behaviors which are difficult to live with. Whenever the parents worry about Marion, Marion is convinced that the parents suffer more than they let on. Although Marion feels that family therapy could help, she also fears that family therapy might be too difficult for the family to endure.*
>
> *Therefore, for the next month, Marion should advertise her difficulties, and the parents' reaction to these advertisements will tell Marion and the family therapists whether the next session should take place. Your next appointment is on Monday, Jan. 3 at 1 p.m.*

This intervention, given at the end of the first session, is a combination of the dance of the seven veils and a prescription of the system which maintains the symptom. The problem in this family was not so much Marion's "condition," but the fact that the family's worry about Marion was the parents' *raison d'être* or favorite pastime. Without this pastime, the couple would have to begin, for the first time, to deal with their rather empty, boring and brittle nest.

Thus, prescribing that Marion escalate her symptoms became the litmus-paper test to see whether the treatment should begin. By telling Marion to escalate her symptoms, we were placing her in a bind. If she escalated she would be conforming to the prescription, which she might not want to do, simply because we told her to do so. In addition, if she escalated, she would be putting her parents to the test of whether *they* really wanted therapy as they claimed. If she did not escalate or reduced her symptomatic behavior, the prescription would have been in the therapeutic direction with respect to eliminating the symptom.

This initial prescription also put the parents in a bind, since it was the parents' reactions to the advertisement of the symptoms which would dictate whether the next session took place (or therapy began). If the parents worried more or chose not to come to the next session, they would be telling Marion and the therapists that the prescription was correct – something they might not want to do, since this was prescribed. If the parents worried less and acted differently after Marion's escalation, this would produce a therapeutic shift in the dance between Marion's symptoms and the parents' worry, and reduce the resistance towards treatment. Thus, paradoxically, only if a therapeutic shift occurred with respect to Marion's showing different behaviors or the parents' showing different reactions to Marion's behavior would there be a signal to the therapists and to Marion that the family was ready to commit themselves to family treatment.

The question of when one needs to employ the dance to capture ambivalent families is complicated. I think the answer to the question comes from the analogical information gathered during the initial interview.

While one is gathering information about the problem during the first session, one is also taking a nonverbal or analogical fix on the family's anxiety about the problem. When the family members are very concerned and anxious about the presenting problem, the dance is not used, since the family is moving towards the therapy and the therapist for help. When the anxiety level is high and there is enough "steam" in the system, one does not have to think about capturing families, since they are already moving in the direction of therapy and change. In these cases the anxiety level is high *and* the family is moving towards treatment.

The dance is also not used when there appears to be minimal anxiety in the family system. When a family comes in to "understand" something that happened years ago and that is no longer a problem, this says to me that there is little leverage for change. Using the dance to activate a system is a mistake and may result in doctor-produced anxiety rather than family-produced anxiety. Therefore, when families come into treatment for insight or understanding, I usually refer them to doctors who do "understanding" therapy. *People do not come in for treatment for understanding — they come in because they are unhappy.*

When, then, does one use the dance of the seven veils? When working with resistant families, one often finds situations where there is a high anxiety level in the family *and* a great deal of resistance to therapy and/or change. The dance attempts to reduce the resistance in the system and direct the family more towards the treatment, the therapist, and towards change. The dance does not motivate, activate, create anxiety, or increase the amount of steam in a system. It is an attempt on the therapist's part to take advantage of a high anxiety situation by reducing somewhat the ambivalence towards treatment and lowering the family's resistance.

CAPTURE BY THROWING DOWN GAUNTLETS, MILANESE STYLE

Another way of capturing resistant families has been described by the Milan Group in their classic work with schizophrenics and anorectics (Palazzoli et al., 1978). The Milan Group captures families by setting up a separate contest between themselves and the family, throwing down an irresistible gauntlet. It is almost impossible for the family not to accept this challenge. However, the therapy is arranged in such a way that, in order for the family to win this second contest created by the therapists, the family system must shift in a way that does away with the need for a symptom.

How does one formulate an irresistible challenge for a family? The Milan Group's gauntlets are based on their understanding of systems, resistance, and analogical information. Irresistible gauntlets also come from their well-developed sense of humor, outrageousness and playfulness, as well as an uncanny understanding of how a particular family works and what in the family must be activated for a successful capture.

The present discussion will refer only to the capturing qualities of the Milan messages; other aspects of these messages will be discussed in other chapters. An example of these Milanese gauntlets will demonstrate how families, particularly resistant ones, are captured.

The Milan Group, Mara Selvini Palazzoli, Luigi Boscolo, Gianfranco Cecchin, and Giuliana Prata, first came to the United States to present their work in 1977 at a conference sponsored by the Ackerman Institute for Family Therapy. While the group was in New York preparing for the conference, my colleagues and I had opportunity to get to know them and to have them consult on some of our cases. We were also asked to find for the Milan Group some difficult families living in New York to interview, so they could then present these families at the conference.

Well, we finally found a difficult family, and it was a doozie — a family of three, with a chronic agoraphobic who had been immobilized in his apartment for the past eight years. In addition, there were reports of violence and threats of suicide, homicide, matricide, patricide, and 32-year-old infanticide.

Gillian Walker and I conducted the initial consultation with this family and then told the family that the second interview would be conducted by the Milan Group, and that the family would benefit from the two Ackerman therapists' getting this consultation.

When the identified patient, Seth, age 32, heard about this upcoming consultation with the Milan Group, his eyes showed great excitement and challenge. Seth then asked whether these experts came from Philadelphia (a well-informed guess); when he was told that they were from Italy and the head of the group was Mara Selvini Palazzoli, Seth indicated that he had heard of her. (This was interesting in light of the fact that this conference was the first time the Milan Group formally presented their thinking in the United States and took place a year before *Paradox and Counterparadox* was published.)

Prior to the Milan Group's live consultation with the family, we showed them a videotape of the first interview which Gillian and I conducted. Palazzoli and her colleagues came up with a hypothesis about this family which was based upon observations of the family's "knee language." The hypothesis and clinical work will not be emphasized at this point, although detailed discussion of this can be found elsewhere (Bergman & Walker, 1983). What I want to illustrate is the capturing quality of the gauntlet which the Milan Group dropped in front of this family.

Ten minutes before the Milan Group was to conduct the consultation with this family, a person describing herself only as a "significant other" called to cancel the session. I was very disappointed because I looked forward to seeing the Group do their stuff with this family.

Instead of showing disappointment, the Milan Group (particularly Cecchin), started giggling, as they often do when families show some of their powerful symmetrical moves. The Milan Group then instructed me to call the family and ask to speak to Seth. Seth was then told that I would spend the canceled hour consulting with the Milan Group and that he should stay by the phone to await the conclusions of the consultation. Four hours later, I called Seth to say that the consultation was too complicated and that the results of the meeting with the Milan Group would be shared with the family at the next session, which was scheduled two weeks later.

The family arrived for the second session, and at the end of the session the message left by the Milan Group for the family was read to them:

We have had a 100% success rate in 28 cases of treating agoraphobia where the agoraphobic was an only child. The common denominator in the cases treated was that the agoraphobic prior to treatment had stayed at home even to the ages of 50 or 60, out of fear that without his presence his parents would fall into a state of intolerable loneliness.

While we were successful in treating the symptom in all 28 agoraphobics, in 10% of the cases we were not successful in preventing the parents from falling into a state of intolerable loneliness. We were therefore relieved when this family chose to stay at home for this consultation, because we felt that Seth had an uncanny sense that his family would fall into that 10%.

> *Respectfully,*
> *The Milan Center for Family Therapy*

There are several capturing qualities inherent in this message to the family. First, the group's use of impressive statistics in an almost "boastful" and "arrogant" way begins a contest which inspires the family towards treatment in order to disqualify the message and prove the experts wrong. Here, *hubris* is being used to provoke the family. There is something about boastfulness and arrogance which compellingly mobilize people to disqualify those who display their pride so openly.

A second capturing quality of the message is the implication that the canceled session served the parents rather than Seth. There is arrogance in this message too, as the Milan Group is saying that they have more knowledge and understanding about why the cancellation took place than the patient does.

The message also implies that Seth canceled the session for the protection of the parents rather than himself. The underlying arrogance that the Milan people are more knowledgeable than Seth and that they know the *real* reason why the cancellation took place further mobilizes Seth towards treatment in order to disqualify the Milan report.

Another "tickle" directed towards Seth's *hubris* is the implication that these experts from Milan have treated many cases and have found that only children remain at home to prevent intolerable loneliness in their parents – even to the ages of 50 or 60. The message subtly implies that a eight-year history of agoraphobia is not that impressive and additionally increases Seth's anxiety by raising the possibility that he could stay with his parents until the age of 50 or 60. This last tickle further mobilizes Seth and his family towards treatment in order to disqualify the therapy.

Finally, the Milan Group's reaction of relief rather than annoyance is a jujitsu move which probably surprised the family. It is likely that the family expects the therapists to be annoyed about the cancellation, which would then provide the family with an opportunity to symmetrically escalate and fight with the therapists, as the family does well with others. Instead, the therapists "duck" and are relieved, which further throws the family's style of embattlement off and leads the family to experience more anxiety because of the loss of their usual control over situations through symmetrical escalation. This increased anxiety provides the therapists with more leverage for treatment.

Thus, in this case, the opening move in the contest began by throwing down a gauntlet, in the form of this message from the Milan Group. The message contained many capturing qualities which moved the family towards the treatment in order for them to disqualify the treatment.

SUMMARY

From the examples cited in this chapter, we see that the first prescription given to a resistant family often contains both capturing qualities and initial strategic moves towards changing the symptom in the system. Without the capturing qualities, which reduce resistance to treatment and enable the therapist to eventually make a contract with the family to begin family therapy, there is a poor chance that they will remain in treatment long enough for change to take place.

Since different ways of capturing families have been discussed in this chapter, one might ask which ones are used under what circumstances and whether certain ways of capturing are more effective than others. These questions are legitimate; I suspect the answers lie somewhere between the almost infinite ways in which a therapist can capture a family and the many ways in which a family will allow itself to be captured. The personal ways in which the therapist connects with the family and vice versa will be based on the personalities and idiosyncrasies of the therapist and the family. There is probably no one correct way for this to happen. Therapists must remain flexible and creative in permitting many ways for therapists to capture and families to connect.

3

FORMULATING
CLINICAL HYPOTHESES

A clinical hypothesis is a tentative best guess or hunch as to why a symptom occurs and how a symptom serves to balance a family system. Here the word "hypothesis" is used in the scientific sense of the word: A temporary guess is formulated and then subsequent data obtained by the investigator either support or refute the hypothesis. When the data do not support a clinical hypothesis, then the initial hypothesis is rejected and a new hypothesis formulated.

When a hypothesis is initially confirmed by some of the data obtained during the treatment session, I usually seek further confirmation by asking more questions. When my hypothesis is confirmed through separate and different lines of questioning, I am then more likely and comfortably able to devise a prescription or ritual as an intervention to change the family. How the family reacts to this initial intervention will in part confirm or refute the initial hypothesis. Usually, the feedback from the intervention will be evident either in the family's nonverbal reactions to the intervention or in a shift in the family system.

Clinical hypotheses have many useful functions for family therapists. One advantage is that the hypothesis directs the therapist toward actively obtaining information about a symptom and the family system in some systematic way. There is very little room for intuiting or "winging it," since clearly important historical and transactional information needs to be obtained from the family. This information will eventually explain how and why a symptom serves a particular system. The information is crucial and decidedly digital in nature. By digital, I am referring to the family's verbal description of the history of the presenting symptom and the solutions they have attempted to eliminate the symptom.

Of course, obtaining this digital information does not preclude tracking analogical information, including all nonverbal behaviors, such as the many forms in which anxiety and resistance are analogically expressed through body language and movement, facial expression, and voice tone in the treatment session.

Another advantage of using a clinical hypothesis is the inherent flexibility in the tentativeness of a particular hypothesis. The clinician's posture here is one of making a guess that will be confirmed or refuted by subsequent data obtained during the interview with the family. There is very little pressure on the clinician to be correct, inspired, brilliant or talented. Sometimes, the personal needs of the clinician to be correct obfuscate further clinical inquiry. With less pressure on the clinician to be correct, there is greater opportunity to be an investigator in a truly scientific sense of the word, where the data from the family system have priority over the needs of the therapist. By calling a hypothesis just that, the clinician remains open to changing the hypothesis whenever different data suggest a different solution to the puzzle.

A clinical hypothesis also permits the therapist to maintain some much needed distance from the family's emotional system. Since the clinical hypothesis needs to be confirmed or refuted, the clinician has his own agenda and is unlikely to be sidetracked by the family's emotional maneuvers. At the same time, however, the therapist must be open to information that contradicts his hypothesis.

How one gathers information to formulate and validate a hypothesis will be discussed in this chapter. My own style comes from the clinical theories of Bowen (1978), the Palo Alto Group (Watzlawick et al., 1974), the Milan Group (Palazzoli et al., 1978), and the work of Milton Erickson (Haley, 1967).

Hypothesizing begins with the initial phone call. While I am talking to the family, I am constructing a rough genogram to get a picture of the family and the symptom. In part I am constructing this genogram to figure out whom to invite to the first session. I am also beginning to hypothesize about what function the symptom may serve in the family. As mentioned in Chapter 1, if the symptom is "small," like bed-wetting, school refusal, or minor discipline problems, I will hypothesize that there is some marital conflict but not of major proportions.

While finding out about the symptom and the family constellation during the initial call, I am also finding out about the referral source and the history of prior treatment. As mentioned in Chapter 1, before formal treatment of the family can begin, the referring contextual issues must be cleared away. If there are problems with the referral, this contextual issue must be dealt with before the family problem is addressed. This will also be addressed in more detail later in this chapter.

When a family presents an impressive history of treatment failures, particularly with competent therapists, I begin to start thinking that change is the last thing on this family's agenda. Perhaps they are coming to me for reasons other than change. It may be to maintain homeostasis; it may be because change was about to take place in some previous treatment and the family dropped out of treatment because of this; it may be because a life cycle change is upsetting a precarious balance. Whatever the case may be, information aids the therapist in formulating an initial hypothesis about the function of a symptom in a family.

One of the things I do when I obtain an impressive history of treatment failure from a family during the initial phone call is to invite more members of the extended family to the first session than I would with a family with fewer treatment failures. There are many reasons for inviting these family members. First, I know that if I am going to change this family, the treatment must be different from what the family expects. I am immediately trying to change the game to which the family is accustomed. If the family agrees, I have a better chance of changing this family than the previous clinician. If the family refuses to do this, then there is nothing lost (at least on my side) and the family always has the option of continuing their game with some less suspicious therapist.

By bringing in more family members, particularly those in the third generation (grandparents), I am playing with more cards in the deck. With the grandparents present in the room, there is less opportunity to present the therapist with the same, conventional, pat story. The presence of the grandparents in the room changes the picture. In addition, the therapist uses the grandparents to verify or disprove the family story.

Bringing in extended family also increases the opportunity for change. One of the assumptions I use in formulating a diagnostic hypothesis is the following: When there is a serious symptom and/or a history of treatment failure, the therapeutic solution to this situation often lies between the second and third generation. If a child becomes asymptomatic and begins to emotionally grow up and become independent, this may, of course, endanger the parents' marriage. However, in addition and sometimes more importantly, one of the parents may be in danger of falling back into an old fused position with his or her parent(s).

The formation of the marriage in the second generation is often an attempt to separate from the parents' parents. The marriage usually doesn't work (because the marital partners never separate* from their parents, grow up first, and then marry), but it does become stabilized by the presence of children. The marriage is tolerable as long as the children remain in the family. Once the children are ready to leave, however, the parents not only risk the shaky marriage but also must begin to deal with old business, namely their fused, angry relationship with their parents. This may be too much to bear. So, although the parents come into treatment because

---

*When I use the word "separate," I am referring to emotional separation or differentiation in a Bowenian (1978) sense.

of their anxiety about their symptomatic child, they are also quite terrified about having to deal with the consequences of their child becoming asymptomatic – having to address their marriage *and* their parents.

By requesting that the grandparents come to the first session, the therapist: a) is bringing in all the main characters; b) avails himself of more information to test the clinical hypothesis, and c) consequently has more opportunity to change the family. The strategy involves clearing the way to deal with some of the old business between the parents and their parents, and beginning separation work between these two generations; then the parents can "let the identified patient go" and get on with the work with their parents and with one another. If the stabilizing forces in the marriage and the old relationship with the grandparents are not loosened, there is little possibility of changing the system in a way that would permit the patient and the other members of the family to progress to their next stages in the family life cycle.

From 1981 through 1984, I have categorically asked three generations to attend the first session whenever the presenting problem is serious (i.e., requiring hospitalization) or chronic (i.e., lasting more than five years). In 90% of the cases, the parents have brought in the grandparents. If the grandparents are deceased, then I seek representatives of the grandparents by asking the parents to bring in their brothers and sisters. Many times the fusion between the parent and the grandparents gets played out through the parent's sibs, so if the sibs are present there is more opportunity for change.

ASSUMPTIONS FOR HYPOTHESIS FORMULATION

In Chapter 1, three assumptions for developing clinical hypotheses were discussed in detail. To briefly review these assumptions, they include the following:

1) All children's symptoms reflect some marital dysfunction.

2) The more serious the child's symptom, the more intense and resistant the marital conflict.
3) The more covert the marital conflict, the more resistant the family system will be to change.

The above assumptions have been helpful to me in formulating more specific clinical hypotheses about why a particular symptom serves a particular family and how I might go about trying to change a family system. Following are some other useful assumptions.

Assumption: You can only be married to one person at a time!

In 1978, I had the opportunity to attend a conference on couples in Florence, Italy. At that conference, I was struck by something Mara Selvini Palazzoli said to the effect that "if a couple comes in for treatment because they are unhappy, and they are connected to their respective families of origin, someone in the family of origin is happy." The implication of this statement is that you can only be married to one person at a time and the spouses are unhappy because they cannot be married to each other because at least one partner is still married to a parent.

Assumption: Marital partners are equally fused or undifferentiated from their respective families of origin.

If one partner in a marriage is still married to a parent, it is quite likely that the other partner is equally married to one of his respective parents. This is an assumption based on Bowen's (1978) notion that partners choose partners who are approximately equal in how differentiated they are from (or fused with) their respective families of origin. Therefore, when a couple comes into treatment with marital problems, I assume that part of their problems comes from the fact that

they are not yet married to each other; rather, they are still
emotionally married to their families of origin. If marriage
therapy is to take place, I usually have to do some divorce
therapy between the partners and their respective families
of origin.

Sometimes, it appears as if one of the marital partners is
less married to his or her parents than the other partner. For
example, it may seem that the wife is more committed to the
marriage than the husband, and her proclamation of this
often puts the husband on the defensive. Here it is important to recall Bowen's (1978) notion that spouses are matched
pretty equally with respect to differentiation from their families of origin. Therefore, if it appears that the husband *is* still
married to his parents, remember that it was the wife who
picked the husband who is still married to his parents. This
gives the wife the opportunity to remain married to her parents, and if she is a good victim, she can additionally claim
being victimized by the husband's emotional unavailability.
This is often documented when I, for example, give the husband some homework involving getting closer to the wife.
This might give the husband the chance to observe how the
wife begins to actively distance from this closeness. By prescribing a task which brings the husband closer, I get the
husband out of the blamed position and rebalance the couple
for couple treatment.

*Assumption: People unable to connect
or form stable relationships with others
are still married to their parents and,
more often than not, to their mothers
rather than their fathers.*

I have found this assumption to be very helpful in all of
my clinical work, which includes working with individuals,
couples, and families, since it explains, with a minimum of
pathologizing, why patients have hard times connecting to
others.

For example, an individual patient comes into treatment

because he or she is isolated, lonely and depressed. I hypothesize that the person is depressed because he or she is isolated and he is isolated because he is still emotionally married to a parent or is deeply involved in the parents' marriage. This allows me immediate direction in the treatment. For example, I might start coaching the patient to act differently with the parent, or I may even call in the parents for a consultation so I can see how the patient is trapped in the marriage and the couple trapped with their child.

If I have to hazard a guess as to which parent the individual patient is more married to (if and when the symptom is not protecting a marriage), I usually pick the patient's mother. I think the emotional attachment to one's mother is greater than that to one's father, although I have seen it the other way, where a great deal of the affective bonding is with a father. I also find that often a patient has overtly or covertly been the mother's confidant or emotional companion during childhood, when father was distant or unavailable.

Assumption: There is no such thing as a dyad.

This assumption also came from the conference in Florence, when Palazzoli (1978), talking about couples, said something to the effect that "there is no such thing as a dyad. The only way you can have a dyad is to parachute a pregnant woman onto an island." What I think she meant by this was that clinicians all too often see the problems as existing in a dyad and forget about the third leg of the triangle that is silent or hidden and that does not appear obviously or overtly related to the presenting problem of the dyad.

Let me just cite a few obvious examples to illustrate the point: When a single parent brings in a symptomatic child who is walking all over the parent, there is *always* a third party involved. The third party could be the ex-spouse, with the symptomatic child bringing the two parents together. Or the third party may be a grandparent, the parent's parent from whom the parent has not emotionally separated. The

symptomatic child may be "protecting" the parent from getting "sucked" back into the parent's family of origin by having
the parent remain focused on the child rather than on her fusion with her parent. A full case study illustrating this hypothesis is discussed elsewhere (Bergman, 1983a). In either
case, the brief family therapist needs to bring these third
parties into the first session in order to create optimal leverage, obtain information, and produce change.

The existence of third parties or third legs of triangles
also becomes clear when a couple comes in for marital therapy. In some cases where it is impossible to treat the couple
directly (because there is some frozen symmetrical power
struggle), an equally viable tactic is for the clinician to think
of possible third legs of the triangle and begin to separate the
partners from their respective families of origin. Perhaps the
symmetrical competitiveness of the couple can be directed
towards some playful contest around who will be able to do
the therapeutic assignments and separate from his or her
family of origin. Thinking of these triangles gets the clinician
out of being stuck in the couple's unproductive symmetrical
struggles.

QUESTIONS ABOUT THE SYMPTOM

Watzlawick, Weakland and Fisch (1974) have provided a
helpful guide to gathering information about a family. The
contribution of this group to my work is the clear set of
transactional and systemic questions which the family is
asked with respect to symptom formation and the solutions
attempted by the family.

By asking questions using what I call the "Palo Alto model,"
I can obtain a *current* picture of the *family members'* perception of how they are organized around a symptom and what
solutions they state they have tried in the past to solve the
problem. I trust the family members' description of how they
are organized *now* around the symptom more than their
perceptions, thoughts, and theories about the *origins* of the
symptom.

The Palo Alto group states that the way in which the family is organized around the symptom is a metaphor for the way in which the family is organized in general. In addition, the family's description of the attempts to eliminate the symptom is again a metaphor for the way in which the family is organized. Thus, from this point of view, there is no need to ask, "How does this family function, or how is it organized?" since the family members will show and tell you this when they describe their history of the symptom and their attempted solutions. Indeed, this is a rather parsimonious procedure in the unparsimonious, ambiguous field of psychotherapy.

The questioning of the family begins with the "naive" question, "Who has the problem?" I address this question, as I do all the other Palo Alto questions, to all members of the family *who speak.* I instinctively do not ask silent members to speak and do not ask them questions until they are ready or *dying* to speak. A therapist who tries to get answers from mute family members will inevitably lose power and respect from the family. Answers can always be obtained from a mute family member by using a Milan version of "gossip in the presence of others" (Palazzoli, Boscolo, Cecchin, & Prata, 1977). This involves asking others in the family, "If Johnny could talk, what would his answer be to the question of . . . ?" People love to speculate on what others are thinking, and the "silent" one cannot tolerate this gossip for long.

"Who has the problem?" is an interesting question, since sometimes there is more than one identified patient in the family, but the person with the presenting problem is the entrance ticket to treatment. The family may present one patient or many. When an entire family sees one member as the only problem, there is usually going to be more resistance to change than when there are several problems, with more than one "patient," or when the family comes for help because of "family problems" (their term). A family with one patient is more frozen in its perception of the problem and will require more powerful interventions by and flexibility from the therapist. For instance, parents who focus entirely on their symp-

tomatic child are in a more frozen system than parents who
focus on their symptomatic child *and also* admit to problems
in the marriage.

"Why is the symptom a problem?" gives the therapist a
quick reading on how much anxiety there is in the system.
Often one finds a disparity between the content of what the
family says is the problem and how much anxiety is shown
by the family nonverbally.

For example, a family might call for an appointment because they are anxious about their son who thinks he is Jesus
Christ. Further questioning indicates that the family is not
upset so much about the son's delusions or psychosis, but are
more concerned about how grandfather, an Orthodox Rabbi,
will react when he finds out that this favorite grandson thinks
he is Jesus Christ. Often the same problem presented by different families produces anxiety for different reasons, and
these reasons must be determined by the clinician, since the
sources of the family's anxiety may not be obvious. Further
questioning of the family about the symptom must focus on
the functional or effective source of the anxiety which brings
the family to treatment.

Questions such as "Does anyone in the family not consider
the symptom a problem?" and "Who is most upset about the
problem?" uncover information about the overt and covert
alliances and coalitions in the family. It is not uncommon for
one parent to be very upset and the other parent less upset
or not upset at all about a symptomatic child. When there
is a disparity in anxiety between the parents, one seeks information about how the symptom bearer is assisting the less
anxious parent. However, one must always also determine
how the symptom assists the more upset parent. *Serious
symptoms* always serve *both* parents, even though initially
it may appear that the symptom is more beneficial to the less
upset parent.

For example, sometimes the patient is one parent's secret
agent who fights that parent's battles with the other parent.

Initially it appears that the patient takes on Parent A because Parent B cannot fight Parent A directly, and it seems like the patient is Parent B's agent. However, under that covert alliance with Parent B often is an even further covert alliance with Parent A, since by fighting with Parent A the patient protects Parent A by making fighting safe (not murderous). It often is the case that the child will protect A because of the myth or reality that B does not know how to fight and so if B started fighting with A, A would be in jeopardy of being murdered. So the patient protects both parent A and B for different reasons and stabilizes the symmetrical battle in the marriage.

Often one sees a similar yet different protective function when a patient keeps the power in the marriage balanced whenever a runaway of power or control threatens the marriage. In this case, the patient with his symptom (often psychotic) keeps one parent from obtaining the upper hand with the other parent by wearing down or defeating the parent who seems to be more powerful at that particular moment. Whenever one side becomes more powerful than the other side, the symptom bearer wears down the more powerful parent until the power in the marriage seems evenly distributed again. Here the patient is the secret agent (and sometimes not so secret and quite noisy) of both parents, and the symptom balances the marriage, rather than the spouses being responsible for balancing their own relationship. A case history which illustrates this balancing is described elsewhere (Bergman & Walker, 1983).

Since the issue of who is really whose agent is usually masked, one of the things I do is to discount the obvious overt alliance and keep on asking myself, "What function does the symptom serve the parent who appears to be the least likely to benefit from it?" With this question, I try to get closer to the hypothesis of how the symptom serves the family system.

When I deal with the question of "Who in the family is most upset about the problem?" I begin to deviate from the Palo Alto model and employ a questioning technique developed by the Milan Group (Palazzoli et al., 1978). This technique involves asking each member of the family to rank order each other family member in terms of who is the most upset to least upset about the identified patient. If one were to ask "Who is upset about Mary's symptom?", social pressure alone would compel each family member to say, "We are all upset." This response gives the clinician no information about the system. However, when family members are forced to rank order who is most upset, followed by whom, followed by whom . . . , these differences give the clinician "differences" that in a Batesonian (1972) manner provide useful systemic information. By asking who is most upset, the clinician is acknowledging that everyone is upset, but some people in the family are more upset than others and these differences are important.

This form of questioning may also be used to obtain other information about the family system. For example, the question may take the form, "Who in the family will remember the patient the longest after the patient commits suicide, followed by whom, followed by whom?" Or the therapist may ask the kids to speculate on how many years mother will remain a widow after father drinks himself to death (with father present in the session), and then rank order their answers as an index of mother's loyalty.

Forcing the family to rank order differences in terms of who in the family is most upset also gives the clinician differences-as-information in terms of who in the family is most anxious.

Next I move to questions about the symptom from the Palo Alto model: "How often does it occur? When? Where? Who reacts to it? In what way?" These questions are addressed to all members of the family, and all answers are welcomed. The importance of getting the transactional information from these questions cannot be overemphasized.

Families come in for treatment with abstract descriptions of the problem, causes, solutions. As long as the therapist stays with the family's abstract description of the family, his hypotheses will be vague and imprecise.

When I am asking these questions, I become "retarded" and "concrete"; I am unable to understand any abstraction. I tell the family that I need a picture in my mind of what happens, what happens next, and then after that, etc. I become a hard-nosed behaviorist, in the best sense of the term, and only accept concrete descriptions of behavior. I emphasize to myself, and to the family, the words "do" and "show." I do not accept "internal states," "interpretations," "states of being," or any other description which I cannot photograph or visualize.

A moment-by-moment sequential picture of when a symptom occurs, how often it occurs, what do people do when this happens etc., is necessary to either validate or refute my ongoing working hypothesis. Families can and will give the therapist these moment-by-moment sequences, but only when he or she insists on such information. More often than not, families will not offer this information if they are not asked. It is important to remember that families do not look at transactions as closely as therapists. They think they are helping the therapist by giving summaries and abstractions rather than descriptions. The more a therapist pursues these sequential transactions, the more information he has to formulate and validate the clinical hypothesis.

"When did the symptom begin?" This is a crucial question. Determination of the month and year of family arrivals (births, adoptions, marriages) and departures (deaths, miscarriages, serious illnesses, divorces) is essential information which must be tracked. Normally, I do a genogram (Bowen, 1978) as I conduct the initial interview with the family. When I look at the origin of a particular symptom, I have been influenced more by Olga Silverstein, Peggy Papp (1983), and Gillian Walker (Morawetz & Walker, 1984) than by the Palo Alto model. By getting a very detailed genogram and tracking dates on important family events (arrivals and departures), one can see how a symptom became overt when some important shift occurred in the nuclear and/or extended family system.

Regardless of the symptom, I have found it useful to look

at generational interfaces when considering the etiology of
a symptom.

For example, in the summer of 1984 I interviewed
a family where the identified patient, Richard, age 25,
had consulted 27 doctors for a problem he has had for
the past five years. The problem, which was reported
by the patient as "foul-smelling flatuses," keeps
Richard from maintaining a job, socializing with girls,
and generally growing up.

During the initial interview with Richard, his parents, and his 27-year-old sister Marion, I construct
a genogram of the family focusing on the symptom.
I learn that the symptom began in 1979, the same
year that Marion got married and father's sister died.
I ask additional questions about how close Marion is
to her parents and brother and how father's sister
was connected to the family. It turns out that Marion
is very close to mother—five years ago, she called
mother each day, and now she calls about twice a
week. Father was close to his sister, but not that
close. The genogram is illustrated in Figure 1.

I learn further that mother has no profession or
career and has basically devoted herself to her husband and children. I also learn that mother and father
separated a few months ago and are in marital therapy with someone else. The spouses trace the beginning of their problems to about five years ago.

I also learn that the flatus occurs usually in mother's presence (in fact, the patient actually flatulates
directly to his mother); that mother has always been
a stickler for good manners, which both father and
son resent; and that father, a sensitive and emotional
man, has a history of keeping his feelings inside until
he becomes explosive and of being unable to express
his anger, particularly to his wife.

With the above information obtained from the initial session recorded on the genogram, my working

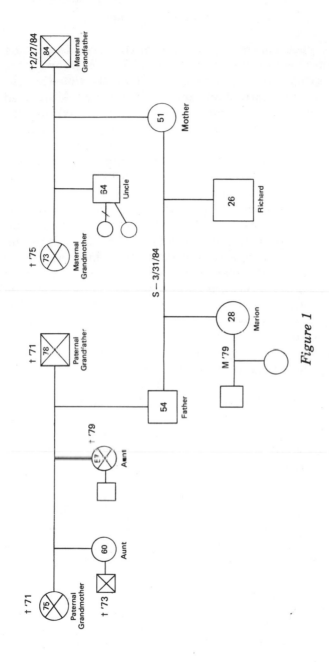

Figure 1

hypothesis for the function of the presenting symptom goes something like this: The occurrence of the symptom five years ago is around the time that the Marion married and father's sister died. Marion (as the first child) was probably triangulated into the marriage by providing closeness with mother and being father's little girl. Following Marion's marriage, the parents' marriage had to be rebalanced, and that rebalancing occurred with Richard's symptoms. The boy's symptom gave mother something to do, since she has defined her main goals in life as being a caring mother. However the son always fights with mother (the way father cannot) and may fight father's battles in the marriage (the patient farts on mother). On the other hand, because of the nature of the presenting symptom, Richard cannot get too close to mother (although he lives with her since father and mother have separated). Understandably, mother cannot tolerate the stench of the foul-smelling flatus. So, in a way, the symptom keeps the son loyal to father too.

Richard is pretty much convinced that his symptoms are organic, although the doctors think not. After the consultation, I tell him that he must continue, perhaps forever, searching for the parasitologist who might find the cause of his foul-smelling symptom. I also point out how his symptom protects his parents and warn that if he were suddenly to lose his symptoms, there would be a "severe whiplash" in the parents' marriage, which might prove dangerous to the parents or to the parents' current marital therapist. Therefore, for the time being he must continue to be symptomatic, perhaps even increasing his symptoms, until he gets signals from his parents that they no longer need his protection.

At the end of the session, I tell the family to give me a call after: Richard has exhausted all medical causes for the symptom; the parents have signaled Richard they no longer need his symptom. Then I will see the family for treatment about once every six weeks. Marion immediately objects because of her job – she lives about an hour away – and Richard becomes furious with his sister for being so "selfish" and "uncaring" about his situation. Richard's expressed fury with sister in this session may have started the changes needed in this system for the symptom to be eliminated.

In this case, there are three-generational reasons for the symptom's occurrences. For reasons still unclear in my mind, the daughter and son have been very involved in balancing their parents' marriage – the daughter by providing closeness with mother and father, and the son by fighting father's battles with mother and giving mother her new *raison d'être*. I assume that the children got triangulated into this marriage because of "incomplete" emotional separations of the parents from their families of origin.

Although the parents' parents are deceased, if and when the family begins treatment I will continue to use this three-generational hypothesis while working with the two generations. I might even do some three-generational work by sending one parent to the cemetery with a tape recorder to "do some work" with his or her parent. What I end up doing will depend upon how rich and clinically correct my tentative hypothesis is, and whether it helps me learn more about the symptom and system. If my hypothesis is not documented over time or fails to direct my line of questioning to more useful systemic information, I will discard the hypothesis and attempt to develop a new one.

"Why does the family come now?" is another question which should be explored during the formulation of the hypothesis. Families have their problems and symptoms for some time before they call for therapeutic help, so finding out why the family comes for treatment *now* rather than earlier is useful. There are many possible answers to this question: The family's attempted solutions are not working so there is increased demoralization; there is greater anxiety in the family system; nonpsychological solutions such as vacations, buying a house, having a child, hypnosis, medical doctors, and drug therapy have been attempted but have failed, etc. Whatever information can be gleaned about why the family comes in now rather than before is systems information which is usually related to the presenting the problem.

"How does the family account for the problem?" is a very rich question, and obtaining each family member's account and explanation of the problem is worth the time and effort. Watzlawick et al. (1974) maintain that often the family's perception of the problem contributes to sustaining the problem. Certainly, my own experience confirms this. However, for me the treasure of this question lies in looking at the thinking styles of the various family members – their "logical" thinking, the color of their thoughts and feelings, and their "language" – namely, the way they perceive and understand their worlds. I use this information later in treatment when I devise a prescription, homework assignment or ritual for the family.

When I do assign a ritual, it will be *in the family's language*. The closer the match between the language of the ritual and the language of the family, the greater the likelihood that the family will act upon the prescription. And the greater the likelihood the family will act upon the ritual, the greater the chances that the family system will change. The family's description of the reasons for the problem gives me an opportunity to plug into their "language."

While I am obtaining information about the family's perception of the problem, I am also asking myself whether the family sees the symptom as "mad" or "bad"; stated differently, "Is the symptom being seen by the family as voluntary or involuntary?" The distinction is important in terms of what the brief family therapist will do to facilitate change. Often "mad" may be reframed to "bad," "bad" to "protective and loving" – the most important thing being that the reframing changes the family's perception of the problem and gives the clinician more clinical leverage and power. For example, if the family sees a child's behavior as "bad," meaning the child is doing something deliberate and has conscious control of the behavior, the therapist might be inclined to reframe "bad" as "sensitive" or "protective of the marital couple."

Sometimes when symptoms were presented by the family as "mad," Minuchin (1974) would reframe "mad" into "bad" by telling parents that their "schizophrenics" were "spoiled rotten kids." The thinking here is that once parents are informed by "experts" that their child is spoiled rather than diseased, in some cases (and I stress some cases, because this will not work in many or all cases), the parents will set up expectations and boundaries for their child which never existed in the past. The therapist then helps the parents maintain these boundaries, come hell or high water. The child repeatedly tests the boundaries and eventually finds himself hitting a "padded wall," so the child "decides" to grow up and get on with his normal rather than schizophrenic life.

At other times, when a family perceives the presenting problem as "mad" or involuntary, the therapist might formulate the problem differently. Here the clinician might make use of hypnotic techniques—making conscious/unconscious splits, splits between the healthy and unhealthy, and splits between "healthy self-interest" and "pathological sacrifice to others."

For example, in the case of the chronic flatulator mentioned above, the family saw the symptom and problem somewhere between medical (parasite) and involuntary/unconscious (mental). The parents overtly and consciously want their son to grow up and live a normal life—so, in fact does the son. No one in this family sees the son as malingering or consciously farting on his mother. Therefore the prescription left with the family went something like:

> *Richard unconsciously has a sense that if his symptoms were to disappear, something terrible would happen to his parents. Therefore, he must continue to protect his parents, at some sacrifice to his life, until he*

*gets signals from his parents that they will be safe if
and when his symptoms disappear.*

This prescription has many components to it. Because the
family sees the symptom as involuntary, so does the therapist. The prescription indicates that the patient's *unconscious*
is protecting the couple – something that cannot be logically
or consciously refuted by the patient or the family. The symptom is then prescribed in order to continue to protect the
couple. Here, one is going with the resistance by setting up
a therapeutic bind. By prescribing the symptom, the therapist is implying that the patient has control over the symptom while telling him to continue doing what he is already
doing. This means that the symptom is no longer involuntary. If the patient goes along with this, he is complying with
the doctor (something resistant patients don't like doing). If
the patient "reacts" to the prescription by not being symptomatic, the "presenting problem" is eliminated.

The prescription also implies that the parents need protection – something that they might have feelings about and
try to change by disqualifying the therapist's prescription.

Then Richard is told that he is sacrificing his life in protection of his parents. "Sacrifice" is a word which most young
adults and particularly schizophrenics hate. I use the word
as often as possible to reframe symptoms, because it is more
positive than family's pathologizing or scapegoating the patient. More importantly, I use the word to mobilize the patient out of that sacrificing position.

Finally, I use the word "signal," which comes from the field
of clinical hypnosis. By telling Richard that he must continue
to fart in protection of his parents until his parents signal
that they are no longer in need of his protection, I am telling
the parents that their son is symptomatic for them and that's
OK. If it is not OK with them and they really want their son
to get better and they really want to change their marriage,
they will do whatever they have to do and this will be a signal
for their son to get on the road.

ATTEMPTED SOLUTIONS

"What has been tried, by whom, and for how long?" focuses on the family's attempts to solve the presenting problem. Like the family's description of the symptom, the way in which the family attempts to solve the presenting problem is a metaphor for the way in which the family is organized. The family's description of what has been tried, by whom, and for how long gives the clinician further information about how the family system is organized. It also tells the wise therapist what he will *not* suggest as a solution for the problem.

"Is there anything the family tried which they feel could have been done more?" is a good question, because sometimes a family comes up with a solution which would have worked if the family continued to use it for a longer period of time. For example, the family became "exhausted" or "bored" or was too "big-hearted" to have the son sleep outside of the house (or with a small child, outside the parents' bedroom). When the parents' solution appeared effective, but they gave up too quickly, the therapist might encourage them to continue more of the same for a while longer. Often, with the support of the therapist the parents are able to continue using their solution for a longer period of time and become successful.

"Do the parents agree/disagree about the solutions?" This question is basically another measure of the differences that the spouses may have in their marriage. Often, differences between partners will come out not overtly in their marriage, but covertly by having "differences in philosophy on child-rearing." Sometimes these differences *are* philosophical and based upon differences in the parents' upbringing, not necessarily marital differences played out as parental differences. When the differences are not marital, then some compromise in the philosophical differences between the parents will be sufficient to shape up the symptomatic child. When these differences are actually marital and the couple stays focused on the parental differences in child-rearing, the symptomatic child will remain symptomatic.

"How do family members react to each other's solutions? Who gets involved, and in what ways?" Answers to these questions give the clinician more systemic, interactive information about the organization of the family and the marriage. If the therapist has done a thorough job getting information about how the family interacts around the symptom, the same systemic patterns are normally seen in the family's description of attempted solutions to the problem. This information may seem redundant, but it also further confirms the ongoing clinical hypothesis. Also, there may be surprises, pointing the therapist in a new direction.

"What would happen if the symptom got better/worse?" This is one of my favorite questions. When the therapist asks, "What would happen if the symptom got worse?", the family is getting the message that it is possible for the symptom to get worse. This sometimes raises the anxiety level in a family, which in some chronic families is not such a bad idea.

All families have the same initial response when I ask what would happen if the symptom got better or disappeared: "Things would be wonderful, lovely, terrific, etc." However, if I persist with this question, sometimes one of the members of the family will suggest a negative consequence which the family might experience after the presenting problem is eliminated. An anorectic girl once told me, "Daddy would be left by Mommy," if she started eating again – and sure enough, *after* Mommy left Daddy exactly one year after treatment ended, the girl started eating.

When families can't come up with any negative consequences following elimination of the symptom, I help them out but asking the same question differently. I may ask, "What would be the danger to this family if the symptom was eliminated?" It is important for the therapist to stress this question and get as much out of it as possible. Usually one or two family members can make some good guesses about the possible negative consequences of change.

Even when the family cannot answer this question, the therapist's asking suggests that he knows that there are likely to be negative consequences to the elimination of the symptom and often the negative consequences will involve the marriage or possibly the nonsymptomatic siblings. The question implies that the family system needs the symptom and the family may have to decide to either learn to live with the presenting symptom or risk having to live with an unknown, perhaps more anxiety-producing symptom. This question also begins to teach the family something about systems and the negative consequences of change.

FAMILY GOALS

Finally, important systemic information is always obtained from such questions as, "What do the family members hope will happen from coming here? What is their ideal goal? What will they settle for? How optimistic are they about improvement? What is the family's history of previous help and the reaction to it?"

Determining what the family hopes to obtain from treatment gives the clinician information about the family members' agenda, their system and their language. Raising issues about the family's ideal goal and what the family will settle for begins to give the family the message that this is *brief* family therapy: We are not going to meet forever to make everyone happy. In fact, it is the brief therapist's responsibility to eventually contract with the family to change a particular behavior in a particular way.

When a brief systemic therapist contracts with a family for a particular goal, the contract should be very concrete and specific. My favorite question in this area is: "What do you want to see the patient *doing* or *showing* two weeks from now that you would call progress or be satisfied with?

A brief family therapist with some common sense does not

contract with the family for goals such as "nirvana," "karma," "existential peaks or heights," "happiness," or for that matter, "everybody getting along better with each other." The latter is not an abstraction or extreme state as are the other mentioned goals, but it is still too vague. I feel more comfortable with goals such as, "In two weeks I would like to see my son fighting less with my husband," or, "In one month I would like to see Johnny have at least a part-time job."

Obtaining a detailed history of the family's hope for change, as well as of previous help and the family's reaction to it, is an important measure of how much resistance there will be in the system for change. In fact, I am so respectful of histories of treatment failures that, when such a history is documented, I immediately begin to prescribe the resistance rather than waste one session by initially prescribing a structural move, even if I have a working hypothesis about why and how the symptom functions in the system.

I assume that the family's previous failures with other therapists/therapies reflect the resistance of the family to treatment, rather than some inherent strength of the symptom. I don't expect to be that much more successful than the past therapists, although, of course, I will not try what other therapists have tried and I will use some things which are new to the family. I will be respectful of the family's resistance and will always take it into account.

For example, in the case of the chronic flatulator, there was a five-year history of the symptom, with the patient seeing or being treated by 27 doctors in the same period of time. With such a history of crusade, I will initially prescribe the resistance and talk to the family about all the dangers of change. There is no good reason for a therapist to make a structural move and have it fail when he should be gathering his power to help the family change.

4

THE USE AND ABUSE
OF TEAMS

THE EVOLUTION OF A TEAM

I have been doing brief family therapy using teams for the past nine years. My first experience with a team began in 1975 during my second year of training as an extern at the Ackerman Institute for Family Therapy. During my first year of training, my fellow externs and I had so much fun with each other that we did not want to be split up into new and different extern groups the following year. The people in this particular group were Richard Evans, Gillian Walker, John Clarkin, Betty Lundquist, and myself.

In addition, during that first year of training my extern group would spend afternoons watching Peggy Papp experiment with new approaches to therapy, based upon the work of Haley and the Palo Alto group. We were also carefully monitoring Olga Silverstein, as she periodically waved her magic wand over difficult couples and families: we were fascinated with her movements.

So, in order to avoid having this first-year extern group of ours broken up, we went to Peggy and Olga and asked them whether they would be interested in supervising us in a second-year externship. Both were happy to do this, and this new group turned out to be the beginning of the Brief Therapy Project at the Institute.

Over the next four years, the original five externs, Olga and

Peggy experimented with different brief therapy approaches. Each year we changed group constellations and alternated supervisors. In 1978, Paul DeBell, Anita Morawetz, and Lynn Hoffman joined the project, and Richard Evans, John Clarkin, and Betty Lundquist left. That was also the first year that we worked without our supervisors Olga and Peggy, who continued to work together and were later joined by Stanley Siegel and Marcia Sheinberg.

In 1979, Peggy Penn joined the project, followed in 1980 by Jeff Ross and John Patten. From 1980 to 1982 the group consisted of Gillian Walker, Lynn Hoffman, Peggy Penn, Jeff Ross, John Patten and myself. In 1982 Gillian and I left this group and asked Phoebe Prosky to join us. Lynn Hoffman, Peggy Penn, Jeff Ross, and John Patten worked together in 1982–83; then Jeff left, then Lynn. By 1984, Peggy Penn and Marcia Sheinberg were working together; Peggy Papp was also working with Marcia; Stanley Siegel, Gillian Walker, Olga Silverstein and I were working pretty much by ourselves.

From 1974 to 1983, Gillian Walker and I worked as team members on about five different teams. During that same time period, she and I have been cotherapists with very difficult families. In 1983, after Gillian and I left our last team, it became clear to us that we too would eventually have to separate. In 1983 we stopped working with each other. Although we still miss working together and respect each other's work enormously, the dynamics between us were clearly getting in the way of the clinical work, and our only solution was to eventually go our separate ways. However, we still consult with one another when one of us gets stuck with a case.

Over the years there have been many advantages and disadvantages of working as a member of a team. There also have been considerable difficulties, which have eventually led to many different teams dissolving and regrouping. Some of the strengths and weaknesses of working with teams will be presented in this chapter.

STRENGTHS OF TEAM WORK FROM
A TRAINING PERSPECTIVE

There is no question in my mind about the usefulness of working with teams as part of a training model for teaching brief family therapy. Being a member of a treatment team for four years provided the richest learning experience in my career as a family therapist.

There are many advantages involved in team training. For me, there were opportunities to learn from both my professional siblings and my supervisors. The team discussions of a case, either before, during, or after a particular session, gave me opportunities to practice and learn to think about systems. When working with a team, all the internal thinking that a clinician ordinarily does in deciding what to do is externalized, examined, and exchanged back and forth before the next clinical step is taken. When there was consensus among team members, this experience led me to feel more secure and confident about my thinking. When there was a lack of consensus, this often led to more rigor in the team and in my own clinical thinking.

Another distinct advantage of learning while working with a team is the continued growth and validation of one's own creativity. I am always much more creative when I am bouncing ideas off others than off myself, and I usually find that group process enhances creative and innovative thinking.

The closest metaphor I can think of comes from my fantasy of what it must of been like when the writers of the old "Show of Shows" got together. Since some of these writers included Mel Brooks, Carl Reiner, Dick Cavett, Howard Morris, Sid Caesar, Woody Allen, and Jack Douglas, my fantasy is that someone would begin a funny story, and then the competitiveness in the group was activated, and someone else would attempt to top the initial story with an even funnier addition to the story or a funnier story. Then someone else would chime in, and on and on. The end result was some of the funniest, most creative sketches ever performed in show business. My sense of team process is that some of that creative, innovative thinking gets activated by a group's or team's process and competitiveness; often the end result is an interpretation or intervention which is very creative and powerful—and probably much more difficult to produce in solo practice.

STRENGTHS OF TEAM WORK FROM
A TREATMENT PERSPECTIVE

There are obvious clinical advantages to working with a team. With a team, there is less danger of a therapist's being pulled into a family's emotional system. The therapist has the freedom to jump into a session, join with the family, play with them, and be assured that the team will eventually devise an intervention which will be therapeutic and powerful.

Another advantage of working with a team is that the combination of therapist and team is always more powerful than a therapist working solo. With very difficult and/or resistant families, a therapist plus a team can present a therapeutic paradox. Usually, the therapist will join with the family, agree with the family's overt agenda for change, and "try" to overtly help the family act upon the overt agenda. The team, on the other hand, will usually address the covert resistance against change in the family and prescribe that the family not change, because, for example, "of the team's fear (*of* the patient's fear) that someone in the family would be endangered if change was to take place."

An example of a split message from a team is illustrated in the case of Elaine, a woman who weighed about 400 pounds and was contemplating surgery to reduce her food intake. Deciding to have the surgery was metaphorically equivalent to emotionally separating from her 450-pound mother.

The following therapeutic split message was offered at the end of the eighth session of treatment:

> *The team believes that Elaine's weight is an amalgam of all of Elaine's subservient roles as sister, daughter, wife, and mother. And were she to give up these*

*subservient roles with respect to all these people, there
would be no real Elaine — leaving nothing! The team
therefore warns Elaine, that because probably no real
Elaine exists, she must always continue to put others
before herself, and therefore never risk losing the
weight.*

*Gillian (Walker, my cotherapist) and I disagree
with the team, and believe that Elaine's recent concern about who she is is an outgrowth of the progress
she has made in asserting herself more. While we
agree with the team that Elaine's weight represents
the burden of all the roles she has been carrying, we
think that as she continues, for the first time, to consider her own needs in a normal, healthy way, the real
Elaine will emerge.*

When working with a team, the therapeutic message can
be totally balanced with a resistant family's message. The
family will say, in effect, "We want to feel better, but do not
change us!" The therapeutic response then becomes, "I, the
therapist, would love to help you, but the team feels that
change would be dangerous in this family." I have found that
the most powerful therapeutic split messages from a therapist and a team occur when there is a real team behind a
one-way mirror; less powerful therapeutic messages come
from using imaginary teams; and the least powerful messages
(sometimes very effective) occur when a therapist without a
team devises a intervention with an internal split message.
An internal split message from a therapist working without
a team might be: "I think with some effort this family can
take the next step, but my experience suggests otherwise."

The use of imaginary teams came about by accident. I was working as a cotherapist with Gillian
Walker, and we were beginning to feel that more resistance was emanating from our team colleagues
behind the mirror than from the resistant family in
front of us. After a while, there was so much resist-

ance from our team that the case was in danger of being sacrificed. We either had to work without the team or blow the case, and we chose the former.

This was a very resistant family, and we had been successfully using split, contradictory messages from the therapist and the team. Since we no longer had the team after the fourth session, and more work needed to be done with the family before termination, we had to come up with something quickly. So we continued to work the way we had for the first four sessions, but took a break from the session, as we would break to consult with a team. However, instead of consulting with the team (which no longer existed), we just consulted with each other. Eventually we returned to the family with two messages, one from "the team" and one from the therapists. This worked out quite nicely, and we were able to maintain the advantages of giving the family a mixed therapeutic message from the team and therapists, while dealing with the resistance generated by the team.

I have come to believe that the power involved in a family's resistance to change must be matched by an equally powerful intervention or interpretation in order for change to take place. At the present time, my sense is that the most powerful interventions occur when a therapist is working with a real team and produces powerful, contradictory therapeutic messages about change to the family.

Another distinct advantage of working with a team has to do with the number of people involved on the team. If four people in the family are needed to develop and maintain their present family problem, four people may be needed to devise the necessary intervention to change this family. The team's power must be equal to or greater than the family's power, and that factor may involve the number of people in each group. However, this is a speculation which I don't want to overemphasize. For example, it could very well be that a team of two experienced, talented therapists is sufficient to balance a family of five people, or a team of two experienced therapists may be equivalent to five inexperienced therapists, and so on.

Another clear advantage of working with a team is the collaboration and support one gets from the team. Difficult families in treatment often escalate in response to a therapeutic intervention. The escalation may immobilize the therapist or lead him and the family to retreat to homeostasis. When there is a team behind the mirror, this escalation is neutralized or creates little anxiety in the therapist, in part because he or she is always consulting with others. Thus, when a family presents the therapist with a malpractice maneuver, or with a suicide-, homicide-, or castration-maneuver, the therapist plus team will not become immobilized as readily as a therapist working alone.

I would like at this point to share a funny story to emphasize how powerful a therapeutic message can be created when working with a team.

A few years ago some of my colleagues and I were visiting the Milan Group in Italy during the summer, when an emergency call came in from a couple in crisis. The couple, in treatment with the Milan Group, had been given the summer off, with the next session scheduled for September. The wife called in a panic, seeking an emergency session because her husband was threatening to castrate himself. The group first consulted with each other and then told the wife that the next session would be in September as scheduled and that the group could not presently help her because her problem was more surgical than psychological. (The couple resumed their treatment in September as scheduled, with the husband intact.)

When certain couples and families escalate to maintain control in the family and of the therapy, a team is crucial to remain meta to the family's emotional system and to keep the therapy directed towards change. In addition, I think a team can devise a "surgical" solution to the crisis more easily than an individual therapist, since each member of a team will have a different reaction to the escalation. The team members' divergent views of a crisis will often lead to seeing an escalation more readily as a maneuver rather than as "real." In addition, the creativity of four team members responding to this maneuver is probably more powerful than any solo therapist's responses. Although I am sure that there are many therapists "out there" who have had enough experience and confidence to see such a threat as a maneuver, I am not sure whether an individual therapist could readily come up with such a powerful counter-maneuver to the castration maneuver.

The existence of a team provides the opportunity to set up a provocative competition, where the family members are challenged to defeat the team but can only do so by giving up the symptom and changing their own system. The team's message challenges the family's hubris and is intended to provoke the family into disqualifying the message with their behavior (Palazzoli et al., 1978). In order to disqualify the team's message, the family must eliminate the symptom — and when the treatment goes well, this is what often happens.

However, it is important to point out that even after the therapy is completed, the symptom eliminated, and the family system shifted, the family may remain furious with the team (Bergman & Walker, 1983). This fury takes some of the "steam" out of the family's system, and this *in and of itself* may have enormous therapeutic effect, since the family may have to reorganize *because* there is less steam in its system. Stated differently, the fury toward the team changes the family's system, since the team is now part of the family system, and having the fury directed towards them implies less towards someone else in the family. This redirection may change the family structure.

This was clearly what occurred in the case of Seth, a chronic agoraphobic, where there was a 15-year history of prior treatment failure before we treated the family in the Brief Therapy Project (Bergman & Walker, 1983). Two years after the treatment ended, a team member called father for follow-up information. Father's rage at the team was as intense two years later as it was at the last treatment session. After raging at the team and the therapy, he let it slip that Seth was greatly improved. Father added that although he " . . . would not give any more information to this team member doing the follow-up, he would be happy to talk with Dr. Bergman, who, in contrast to the team, was a good and caring person who could have helped the family if he had been allowed to see them without the team."

By virtue of the intensity of father's feelings about the team and the therapy two years after treatment ended, it was clear that the team indeed had become a "member" of the family and the target for some of the rage in the family. The redirection of some of this rage may have helped clear the way for a shift in mother and father's marital relationship, which in turn may have shifted the family system to no longer requiring intense agoraphobic symptoms to balance the family system.

I doubt if many individual therapists could stay connected to a family while having this kind of fury directed toward them. A team is probably necessary to receive this fury while the therapist stays on the family's side of the competition.

WEAKNESS OF TEAM WORK FROM
A TRAINING PERSPECTIVE

Recently I have had an opportunity to teach the third year of a three-year program in brief family therapy. The students have been trained using a team model, and it is quite clear to me as a teacher what the advantages have been of this training. Also quite evident are some of the shortcomings of using a team approach as a training model.

The first and biggest problem is the dependency that a student-therapist can develop when trained with a team. Also, although there is no contradiction between learning how to do therapy with a team and developing one's own style, confidence, and independent thinking when working solo, this does not always happen.

One of the dangers of the supervisor/team knocking on the door or calling in frequently is that the student-therapist will become dependent on a team or supervisor to come up with powerful interventions. At first this is probably necessary. However, it is crucial that the supervisor/team let the student swim, coming into the treatment in progressively smaller ways over time. Within a team format, the power of the team, as well as the student's own style, confidence, and independence, should be used to help the family change. Perhaps team training is most helpful for somewhat experienced therapists who have already developed some sense of style, ability to use self, and role confidence.

WEAKNESS OF TEAM WORK FROM A TREATMENT PERSPECTIVE

Intra-team dynamics can have potentially deleterious effects on clinical work with families. One of the things I do naturally (which is both a blessing and a curse) is track process dynamics. When I was a member of a team or a therapist working with a team, I would track the process between the family and the therapist, the therapist and the team, and the intra-team process. When I worked as a cotherapist, I would track the process between the cotherapists and the family, between the cotherapists and the team, between the cotherapists, and among the team members.

When there is little conflict or anxiety between the cotherapists or between the therapists and the team or within the team itself, you have one of the most powerful and effective forms of treatment, particularly with difficult and resistant families. When things are not right between the therapist and the team or within the team, the dynamics of the therapists and team "take over" and influence the clinical thinking of the therapy in a way that is more often negative than positive. That is, when the therapists are all right, the treatment is free to proceed, and when the therapists are not all right, the treatment is postponed. This is based upon my belief that therapists have to take care of themselves or be unencumbered by their own dynamics before they are free to help others with their dynamics. A good schizophrenic will amplify a preexisting split between two cotherapists in the same way that this patient will amplify a split between two parents.

From my perspective, when a split occurs within a team or between a team and therapist or between two cotherapists, these dynamics must be dealt with first—before the therapists are free to resume treatment. To make believe that everything is OK or to get into heavy-duty "process" discussion is usually a pseudo-solution. Many of the teams of which I have been a member have *not* dealt directly with dysfunctional process in the team/therapist system. Eventually such teams dissolve because the treatment becomes ineffectual or the work becomes boring and unpleasant.

What are the difficulties within a team or between two cotherapists which eventually lead to short team life spans? I suspect the issues are not unlike those that occur in families and couples. (Of course, what is interesting is how many times professionals who are "experts" in solving couple and family problems are unable to recognize these phenomena when they occur in their own work situation and how this lack of recognition leads to poor clinical work and/or the dissolving of so many groups.) When a team goes astray, the issues are likely to involve balance, reciprocity, complementarity, symmetry, validation, *quid pro quos* and competition—just as in families.

When I was an student-extern and working with a team, my role and function on the team were clearly defined. I was a good, responsive student to my supervisors who led the team; I was learning, they were teaching, and the complementary was clear. I was also the funny, outrageous and quirky one, so I had a special role and function on the team. This worked well for a few years, until the complementarity of the relationship I had with my supervisors changed. I became more confident, more independent, and less needy of my supervisors' guidance. Eventually, this led to my going off with some of my professional "sibs" to form a new team.

This shift was a natural developmental change, much like the changes which occur in a family when a child grows up, becomes adolescent, and eventually "leaves home." I might add that, although I haven't worked with my initial supervisors in the Brief Therapy Project in five years, I still feel high regard, respect, and affection for them. Now we operate more like peers: We refer families to one another, ask for consultations when we are stuck, and maintain an affectionate and respectful relationship. Both historically and affectionately, they will always be my professional "parents," but now our therapeutic styles are different – and that's OK.

Some of the difficulties I experienced on a different team involved issues of balance, validation, and competition. This was a team of six therapists, paired off into three sets of cotherapists, each with a male and female therapist. My partner was Gillian Walker, who had been my cotherapist for eight years.

There were too many imbalances for this team to function as a cooperative six. The other two cotherapy teams had not worked as partners as long as Gillian and I had, so they had to learn about each other and develop a way of working together. Gillian and I were like an old married couple; we had worked out our complementary roles and knew how to avoid stepping on each other's feet. Because we had the oldest and relatively most functional "marriage," we were the strongest therapist couple. In addition, we had more clinical training and experience than the other four. This combination of experience and "marriage" made us more powerful and successful with the families we were treating.

Our therapeutic successes bred resentment and competition in some members of the team. If the other, less experienced members of the team could see themselves as students (as two members did), this complementarity would have rebalanced the team and everyone would have gained something from this experience. The problem was that another member of the team, although less clinically experienced than Gillian or myself, was a well-known family therapist, who could not tolerate being in a inferior position to us in a clinical setting. The covert competition was so enormous and intense that it affected the whole team. If given the opportunity, this well-known therapist would, of course, express a different and probably legitimate point of view.

When a team becomes absorbed in and upset over its own stuff, there is not much energy left for creating powerful and effective interventions with families. While Gillian and I were taking on very difficult, resistant families, things became so bad with the team that we both felt there was more resistance behind the one-way mirror than in front of it. In order to keep the treatment moving we eventually left the team and finished the cases without them, using an imaginary team. The cases then went quite well, and the follow-up information about these families was good. I have not fully recovered from the aftermath of that team experience. There is still a somewhat bitter taste in my mouth.

One risk of destructive competition within the team is the unconscious impulse to "blow" the case in order to maintain or regain some balance within the team. Experienced family therapists are aware of the self-sacrificing lengths identified patients will take to insure balance in their own familial contexts. Similarly, a therapist may become a "failure," sacrificing both his competence and the family's chances for change, to take the heat off the team family. When a team member senses that such dynamics are affecting his clinical work, it is time to deal with the issues in the team; if these cannot be resolved, the team should be sacrificed, rather than the family.

Another potential danger of team work is the tendency to devise *overkill interventions*. There are times when a very simple intervention or interpretation is needed to help a family change. Sometimes that very simple intervention is not available because a team of four members may be "too powerful and complicated" to come up with a simple intervention. The team takes on a life of its own and may need to come up with clever, powerful interventions to justify its existence.

One of the common and frequent errors I observed when working with teams was when the team was more powerful than the family and proceeded to devise interventions which were based upon the team's cleverness rather than the family dynamics. For example, there were times when paradoxical interventions were used when there appeared to be very little family resistance, and when simple structural interventions would have worked. Other times the clinical hypothesis and treatment became more complicated than was needed because the team was more in need of complexity than was the family.

Unfortunately, the family's treatment may assume a backseat to the team dynamics. One way to avoid this is for one member of the team to track team process and to make determinations before treatment starts about whether a team is really needed with this particular family. It has also been my experience that when I do cotherapy with a family I can readily treat without a cotherapist, the cotherapist and I start "walking" all over each other. In other words, there must be enough work and roles for two therapists; when there is not, the cotherapy can produce as many problems as the family.

INCREASING THE LIFE SPAN OF A TEAM

During a conference on brief therapy with difficult families (Bergman, 1981b), I spoke about the advantages of team work. I mentioned the unfortunate short life span of a typical team. In a half-serious and half-kidding way, I made the following recommendations for increasing the life span of teams:

1) Assign a different member of the team to be the team's scapegoat for that particular month and change scapegoats on an even and regular basis.

2) Work with the most impossible, resistant, and terrifying families, i.e., take the competitiveness out of the team and redirect it toward the family.
3) Form a strategic team in the most orthodox psychoanalytic institute to be found in any city. Working in a unvalidating, hostile context will always keep a team together longer.
4) Choose team members on the basis of brain development. Each member should have a uniquely developed part of the brain. An ideal team would have a left hemisphere person, a right hemisphere person, a midbrain person, and if possible, a brainstem person.

5

VICTIMS, KILLERS, AND SNIPERS

This chapter explores strategic ways in which victims can be coached out of their painful positions. The diagnostic and etiological thinking is mostly Bowenian (1978), and the theory of change comes from Bowen Theory as well as from the work of the Milan Group (Palazzoli et al., 1978), Milton Erickson (Haley, 1967), and the Palo Alto Group (Watzlawick et al., 1974).

Bowenians might criticize these interventions as being too reactive and suggest that patients should learn to be even less reactive (emotional), which over time would produce shifts in other parts of a family system. This criticism is probably valid. However, the interventions described in this chapter are, for me, powerful, fun, playful, and alive. And the end result of both approaches may be the same, namely, differentiation and enjoying closeness in more authentic ways.

The more I do psychotherapy and think about systems, the more I see patients taking victim positions. The victim position involves seeing oneself as helpless, pained, hurt, impotent, fearful, naive, honest, and usually reactive to some other person, often seen by the victim as the "killer." In addition, victims usually show vulnerability, are very sensitive to others, place other people's needs before their own, and are more in need of approval from others than they are able to give themselves approval.

Victims suffer for a number of reasons. They feel enormous anger, frustration, and pain, and since victims are unable to directly express or handle these feelings, there is often rage. The anger, frustration, and pain are often the end result of taking a victim position, namely, feeling deprived, seeing people they do things for as ingrates, and often not knowing what they want or who they are, since victims are usually more tuned into others than themselves. Since the anger, frustration, and pain are not often overtly expressed, the therapist may have to deal with such indirect expressions as psychosomatic complaints and disorders, depression, and passive-aggressive guerrilla-war tactics.

The "killer" is usually as vulnerable and insecure as the victim – or more so – but his vulnerability and insecurity are hidden or expressed in behaviors which are viewed by the victim as cold, aggressive, tough, attacking, snobbish, omniscient, perfect, never admitting vulnerability or pain, emotionally inexpressive, calculating, or selfish.

One other position that should be described is that of the "sniper." When snipers are unable to contain insurmountable buildups of frustration and anger, they usually snipe when others are vulnerable or not looking. In "reality," killers and snipers are victims too. The killer masks his or her vulnerability by appearing invulnerable. The sniper, unable to contain buildups of anger, snipes periodically. For the purposes of this chapter, although killers and snipers may appear to be people, or types, or positions taken by people, they are best understood as a classic victim's *perception* of others in a social context. Whether they are real people or positions is less important than the victim's view of them as out there and having the potential and ability to cause the victim pain.

SOME INDULGENCES IN LINEAR THINKING

From my clinical work, I get the distinct feeling that victims evolve from being subjected early in life to an offensive environment. This offensive context can come, for instance, from a parent's taking anger out on a child rather than a spouse, from a child's becoming an identified patient to draw attention from a marriage, or from a child's being raised in a setting where there is murderous marital tension or where conflict cannot be expressed and therefore resolved. In many cases, in order to protect himself or herself from this offensive setting, the child withdraws emotionally or physically. This is one of the early steps in becoming a good victim.

In time, this reflex to withdraw becomes a pattern used in dealing with other forms of anxiety in social contexts, and the victim learns to withdraw, react (rather than act), and/or defend. Safety becomes more important than satisfying other needs. Power is imbued by victims in others, since victims see others doing things to them and do not see that they are participating in a victim-killer collusion. Since victims react rather than act, they seldom say what they want or actively seek to satisfy their own needs. As a consequence, victims feel enormously deprived, and this deprivation is a major source of frustration, anger, and perhaps rage.

One of the goals of treatment with victims is to give them the experience of being out of this one-down position they have experienced most of their lives. Once victims, through therapeutic coaching, experience being in a one-up or parallel relationship with others, they start enjoying and experiencing their power, rights and privileges. They are then able to be more active in social contexts and to begin getting more of what they want. In addition, by coaching victims out of the one-down position and teaching the politics of relationships, therapists can help victims become more responsible for themselves, start taking more "I" positions, and stop participating unwittingly in victim dances with others.

VICTIMS IN CONTEXT

Besides looking at people's potential for assuming victim positions, one must also consider the interpersonal context in which "victimization" takes place. Jackson's (1968) description of the three major relational contexts deserves some mention at this point.

One can be in a one-down position in a complementary relationship where there is overt or covert mutual consent between two people. "I will be helpless, and you will take care of me," could be a covert or overt agreement which works for a couple. In a parallel relationship, there is some alternation of one-up and one-down positions in different areas of a couple's relationship. "I will be helpless and you will take care of me in area A, and you can be helpless and I will take care of you in area B." In these cases, the one-down positions are distributed in some agreed upon way, and the individual is not too one-up or too one-down for too long in the *relationship*. There is a *quid pro quo* operating in these relationships, with a tacit agreement that the power and control in the relationship are equal and balanced from the partners' point of view.

"Victimization" begins to occur in symmetrical relationships when there is little or no agreement between the partners on the various one-up and one-down positions in the relationship. Two one-uppers may fight for control in one-up positions, or two one-downers may fight for control in their down positions. In such symmetrical battles, there is little consent or agreement on the positions people take, and both partners end up feeling like victims.

Sometimes there is an escalation between two one-downers where A takes a one-down position, B one-ups A by taking a further one-down, which is further escalated when A one-ups B once again, etc. The end result of this symmetrical escalation is that the winner victim is able to take the most extreme one-down position and stay in charge only by maintaining a serious disease or by dying. This sort of dance has been aptly termed "sacrificial escalation" by the Milan Group (Palazzoli et al., 1978). For example, it is not uncommon to observe a couple in sacrificial escalation where the wife begins with back trouble, followed by the husband's developing an ulcer, followed by the wife having ulcerative colitis, followed by a coronary for the husband, followed by cancer of the colon for the wife, followed by death for the husband. In such cases, the winner is the loser and the loser is the winner. A rather nasty game for control!

Quite often, when working with couples, I notice how victimization is balanced in a relationship by one partner's taking an *overt* victim position, while the other takes a *covert* victim position. The covert victim might try to control with guilt and passive-aggressive guerrilla-war tactics, while the overt victim might control with complaints, nagging, pushiness, or aggressiveness. What usually happens, after a while, is that each feels victimized by the other. They then try to get out of their victim positions by trying first-order rather than second-order solutions (Watzlawick et al., 1974).

In treatment, one of the things I do to break this cycle is inform the spouses that they are *both* victims in this emotional dance, and that neither has an understanding of – or any control over – their dance. One of the goals of treatment is to teach them how they can take charge of the dance, rather than allowing the dance to control their relationship. This approach often joins the couple with the therapist in a mutual fight to stop their victimization by each other and the emotional dance, and to take charge in a new, nonvictim way.

HELPING VICTIMS CHANGE

When working with victims, I find it helpful to point out to them that they are taking a victim position. Many victims are unaware of the position they are taking or have never conceptualized their behaviors as falling into victim positions. There are several therapeutic consequences of pointing out victim positions to people:

1) Since victims are so reactive to begin with, the very act of pointing out the position they are assuming begins to mobilize patients out of this position.
2) Emphasizing that a person is *assuming* a victim *position* is hopeful, since it implies that the suffering is of a temporary nature and that the person eventually will have some control over whether victimization occurs.
3) Underscoring to victims *how* they participate in becoming victims gives them, once again, a sense that they have some opportunity or option to act differently.

I was once told by Betty Carter* that the world was never conquered by people who assumed victim positions, and that statement has stayed with me a long time. As a consequence, I point out to patients that from their victim position they are much more in charge of avoiding what they do *not* want than of getting what they *do* want. Hearing this statement has been helpful in mobilizing victims out of their position.

Now, there are always major league victims who will not respond therapeutically to being told that they are assuming victim positions. After all, some professional victims might deny that they are victims. With this population of people, I hammer away, trying to show them how they are being victims. Sometimes, this persistence works.

When this does not work, I then go with the resistance. I might, for example, point out how a patient's adherence to this position shows loyalty to a parent in some protective way. As long as a patient suffers from being a victim, he might continue to make his parents feel needed as parents. Or, a victim might also stay loyal to her parents by insuring that she remains as unhappy as or unhappier than her parents, because if the victim were to become happier than the parents, she would be overwhelmed with guilt. Prescribing that the victim continue to assume this position sometimes mobilizes him or her out of this position — as long as the prescription is accurate and framed in effective language.

I sometimes give a resistant victim a powerful ritual to perform. I tell him to find photographs (preferably enlargements) of his mother and father and each night to "tell" these photos what he did (or did not do) that particular day to insure that he remained unhappy or less happy than his parents. Then he is to say that he did these things for his parents and that he wanted them to know this. Often this ritual mobilizes the victim out of this position.

If and when the victim agrees that he is assuming a victim position, I begin to coach him by giving him homework assignments or rituals. "Cooperative" victims need to be coached and encouraged to practice getting out of their posi-

---

*Personal communication, 1981.

tions. Because of my own needs and style, I often try to make the homework funny and outrageous. Usually the quality of the patient's laughter indicates the level of anxiety which will emerge in the system once a victim begins to take a different position. My experience suggests that the humor and outrageousness of the assignment begin, in the treatment session, to detoxify some of the anxiety which will be associated with change. In addition, if I present a Hobson's choice of two outrageous alternatives, the patient will usually decide to choose the less outrageous assignment or will come up with his own alternative. The task which the victim finally chooses is usually sufficient to begin getting him out of this position.

A patient was complaining one day that whenever he and his wife have dinner with his parents, he always feels anxious. Further inquiry revealed that somehow he always finds himself sitting next to his mother, whose hand always winds up on his thigh. For "inexplicable reasons," my patient becomes very anxious and doesn't know what to do, for fear of offending his mother.

The assignment I gave to the patient was this: The next time he had dinner with his folks and his mother started feeling him up, he was to gently guide her hand towards his crotch. As one could imagine, the moment this assignment was given, there was enormous laughter. Instead of following through with the assignment, the next time he had dinner with his folks, and I believe ever since then, he has become quite active in insuring that he sits next to his wife (with whom he now plays under the table) and away from Mama.

* * * *

Another patient felt quite overwhelmed and victimized by his recently divorced mother, who lived in Cleveland. He was an only child and the only close connection to mother. Although mother had several sisters (whom she "hated") living in Cleveland, she would call her son in New York many times in the middle of the night because she was feeling suicidal or having a crisis. The patient's father was living near the mother and was still interested in remaining friendly with her, but mother wouldn't hear of it because she was still furious over the divorce. Mother's emergency calls not only terrified my patient, but also began to disrupt his relationship with his live-in girlfriend.

The homework assignment I gave to this patient was as follows: The next time mother called in a crisis, he was to take a one-down position. Normally, he would try to help, advise, console mother – all to no avail. His one-down position was to *show* panic and helplessness. After finishing the call to his mother, he was instructed to call his father or aunts (mother's sisters) and ask *them* to help *him* with his anxiety over mother's calls.

This assignment, if acted upon, would have clearly done the trick and changed the dance which formerly placed my patient in a victim position. My patient laughed for a while, and then declared that he could not do this homework – he loved Mama too much; she was too vulnerable; she would never speak to him again; I, the therapist, did not understand how much he loved her, how big she was in his life, etc. I then dropped the assignment.

At the next session, he once again was panicky and terrified about his mother's welfare because of the middle-of-the-night phone calls. This time I told my patient that he basically had two options: He was to either do the homework assignment I gave to him the week before, which he could not do at that time, or fly out to Cleveland and sleep with his mother, which he always fantasized about doing. That way he could get the incest over with; then he would be able to get on with his life.

The patient seriously considered the idea of flying out to Cleveland with his incestuous fantasies (which absolutely floored me). Instead, the next time mother called in the middle of the night, he chose to do the original homework and to call his father *and* mother's sisters.

My patient married his former girlfriend a few months later. Mother refused to attend the wedding, but two years later we find her alive and well in Cleveland and calling her son on Sundays about twice a month.

HELPING VICTIMS HANDLE KILLERS

When treating victims, it is important to find out where and how they find themselves in one-down positions with respect to perceived killers. There is invariably something, sometimes quite subtle, the victim sees the killer doing, that makes the victim feel insecure. This must be closely tracked by the therapist. The moment this dance is understood by the therapist, usually some reversal of position or response, correctly framed, will be sufficient to help the victim out of his accustomed position.

One reframing that I have found to be helpful and powerful is to tell the victim that the perceived killer is probably even more insecure and vulnerable than the victim and that the killer's actions are probably the result of his or her vulnerability. (Victims seldom see the killer as vulnerable or insecure.)

For a reversal to be effective, the reframing assignment must make the victim relatively *active* rather than *reactive* with respect to the killer. Victims are accustomed to reacting to their killers, which automatically begins to place them in one-down positions. They almost reflexively go into reverse gear. A reframing assignment should prompt the victim to take on the killer actively in first or second gear.

In assigning reversals to victims, three other factors should be emphasized. First, the therapist must find out how important the killer is to the victim and whether the victim wants to stay connected to the killer. If the perceived killer is an important person, such as a spouse or employer, then helping the victim out of his victim position is indicated. If the perceived killer and victim have no future in common, and the victim is not interested in staying connected to the killer, then the homework assignment might involve coaching the victim into gracefully or playfully disconnecting from the killer. Contrary to what many victims believe (that they must be liked by everyone), there are joys and benefits in having enemies. It is important for the victim to learn how to disconnect from people whom he or she considers unimportant or offensive.

The second issue to be kept in mind when coaching victims in dealing with killers is that of timing. Usually, the less reaction time the victim takes in responding to the killer's attack, the better. Nipping an attack in the bud reduces self-pity and brooding time for the victim and signals to the killer that the old attacks will no longer work. Generally, after an attack the victim, much later, thinks of a better response or a more powerful reversal, but then it's too late and the victim knocks himself for being stupid. In treatment, I encourage my victims to practice their homework and at the same time to try and reduce their reaction time. The closer the reversal follows the attack, the better.

The third factor involves the effectiveness of "straight" or direct approaches in this particular relationship. Before I assign reversals to victims, I usually test the waters to see whether a direct approach will stop the killer attacks. Victims are encouraged to respond to an attack with such statements as: "That's hurtful!" "Ouch!" "You can't talk to me this way!" "Stop attacking me!" Sometimes this is heard by the killer, and nothing more is required.

When such cries are not heard or respected by the killer, a more powerful intervention, such as a reversal of the victim's response or position, is needed. This reversal is usually specific and based upon the anxiety the victim experiences in relation to the perceived killer. If, for example, a victim becomes anxious because the killer is perceived as cold, I would encourage the victim to be affectionate, warm, or embracing (putting an arm around the killer, squeezing his hand, neck, etc.). The reversal certainly does not warm up the killer (although it might), but it transfers the anxiety from the victim to the killer. After the reversal, the coldness no longer produces anxiety, and the victim no longer feels in a one-down position. At this point the killer might become anxious because the level of affection (closeness) is now being controlled by the former victim. Victims are usually astonished over how a hug might pop a killer out of his chair. The whole thing is rather powerful and dramatic to them.

Another example of helping victims by coaching them to use reversals comes from my own family. A few years ago, my younger brother called me to complain that my mother was calling him at his office five times a day, and that he was now ducking calls and hiding behind the switchboard operator and his secretary. He didn't know what to do and was asking me for advice.

Earlier that year my folks had decided to retire to Florida, but agreed that, while my father would remain there, my mom would continue working in New York four days a week. On weekends she would fly to Florida to be with my dad. It soon became apparent that while in New York she was very lonely. As a result she began to call my overwhelmed brother, continually interrupting him at work.

The task I gave my brother was the following: He was told to call my mom's office eight times a day to chat, schmooze, ask for advice, using any excuse to give a ring. On the eighth call, he was to tell her that he had nothing to say, but that he was about to leave his office and was afraid that my mom was going to call and would miss him.

My brother did the assignment for three days, and at the end of the third day my mother angrily told him that he was a big boy now and could begin solving his own problems and that she was too busy in her office to be interrupted so often by his calls. After that my mother called my brother only once a week, which was exactly the amount of contact with her that he wanted.

Clearly, my brother felt victimized by the calls which put him in a one-down position. He was distancing; my mom pursuing. He was hiding; my mother searching. He couldn't tell my mother to cut it out, because he was still getting caught up in his need for her approval.

Why was the intervention successful? First, through use of this reversal, my brother was placed in charge of the phone dance rather than my mom. Second, my brother's asking my mother for advice is consistent with his last-born position in the family; more importantly, however, it restructures the definition of the relationship as one of a younger son asking advice from mother, rather than a mother looking for closeness with a pseudo-husband-son. Finally, the last call was probably toxic to my mother's *hubris*, since it redefined my brother as being in a one-up position to her, since he was anxious that she would be upset at not reaching him if he had left the office for the day. In effect, he told her on the eighth call that he was anxious about her anxiety. This placed him in the superior position, an intolerable situation for her. She resolved my brother's problem by telling him to grow up and by calling once a week rather than five times a day.

Another reversal I find effective is used for victims who see their killers as aggressive, angry, attacking, or blaming. I encourage the victim, after he receives a shot from an attacker, to convert the killer into a mental patient with earnest, sympathetic questions, such as: "Are you all right?" "Is everything OK?" "Is something wrong?" When the killer responds

with, "Of course everything is OK. Why do you ask?" the victim gently and sympathetically says, "You seem so upset, unhappy, and I thought that maybe something was wrong, or
that maybe you wanted to talk about it." This last response
is a not uncommon one-up maneuver used by some psychotherapists with their patients to maintain control; it is certainly effective in helping the victim get out of his position
with respect to an attacking killer.

HELPING VICTIMS HANDLE SNIPERS

Snipers are much more difficult to handle than killers, part-
ly because they are more difficult to identify. Snipers only
strike periodically, when they can no longer contain their
anger or rage; also, more often than not, they strike out of the
blue, when least expected. They also strike so fast that victims are often unaware of being attacked until a considerable
time later. Only then, when there is little opportunity for re-
course, does the victim start fuming.

One of the first steps in handling snipers is to identify
them. Snipers come in all forms, including victims and killers.
After a victim has experienced a few unpredictable, inexplicable snipes, which appear to come out of nowhere, he begins
to identify this individual as having sniper potential.

The next step in dealing with snipers, as with killers, is to
decrease the reaction time of the victim in responding to the
snipe. The faster the reaction time, the better, since it immediately signals to the sniper that he has been identified and
that the victim refuses to be a target.

The classier and more elegant the victim's response to the
sniper and the faster it occurs, the more the victim gets out
of a one-down position and places himself in either a symmetrical or one-up position to the sniper. It takes time and practice to recognize snipers, reduce reaction time, and come up
with responses to neutralize snipes.

My personal preference for responding to snipers is to use
confusion and humor. Often, after a sniper's attack, victims
feel so confused or hurt that they cannot respond well. Be-

cause they are so upset they cannot think, and because they cannot think the reaction time of their responses is a few days longer than they would like it to be. Consequently, I suggest a response which does not require thinking. What I do after being sniped, and what my patients have done with considerable success, is to kiss the sniper on the nose, giving no explanation. People know immediately when they are being sniped, and although they cannot react fast enough to think, they can react fast enough to kiss a sniper on the nose.

The kiss does several things. First, it provides an immediate (and therefore powerful) reaction to the sniper. Second, it probably confuses the sniper, since the last reaction to the snipe he expects is affection. Third, responding to a snipe with affection has a "forgiving" or a "forgive them for they know not what they do" quality about it. Thus, both the confusion induced in the sniper and the forgiving posture move the victim from a potential one-down position to an almost double one-up position. As a consequence, snipers might think twice the next time they snipe. They may choose to stop sniping with an informed victim or choose to search for less-informed victims.

An example of the use of humor to neutralize a sniper comes from my own experience with a psychotherapist-sniper. My colleague and I were doing some training at the Ackerman annual conference in the country. At a cocktail party one evening, my colleague said she wanted to introduce me to her ex-therapist, who was at the training workshop with his wife, who was attending the conference. My colleague was excited about introducing me (her cotherapist for about seven years) to this man (her therapist for five years).

After she introduced me and her ex-therapist, the first words out of his mouth were, "What are you?" Not "How are you?" or "Who are you?" but "What are you?" I was truly taken aback, confused, and a bit hurt. I recovered and responded, "An Aquarian." The therapist mumbled something to mitigate my response, but it didn't have the clout of the Aquarian response. Only my colleague's upbringing kept her from rolling on the floor with laughter.

I think the reaction time of the response and the recovery with humor were the most important factors in neutralizing this attempted sniper attack. It is also very powerful and amusing to handle a therapist sniper attack by getting into astrology (and changing turfs).

Another example comes from my experience giving workshops or conferences, where sometimes I am challenged to deal with a multitude of potential snipes.

For the past few years, I have noticed a pattern which develops when I go out of town and conduct a two-day workshop in brief family therapy. Usually after lunch on the *second* day some sniping occurs over my presentation, whether it be the clinical theory or the videotapes. At first I am usually confused and hurt, because it appears that the workshop is going well. The audience is appreciative, involved, and sometimes excited, and the presentation is clear, energetic, and humorous.

I was complaining one day about this to my therapist, Ian Alger, since I was anxious and confused about what was happening. Ian's suggestion did the trick. What I did after lunch on the second day was to begin the afternoon session by telling the audience that I have a peculiar quirkiness which I must share: I feel that I have done a terrible job as a workshop leader if after a day and a half of training I haven't pissed off a few people in the audience. And now, I add, I would like to spend some time answering questions and having some discussion with some of the people I have pissed off.

Later I realized that in presenting a workshop I was in a dilemma and certainly in a no-win situation. My own naiveté kept me from realizing that I was being sniped at by some people *because* I was leading a successful workshop, and their competitiveness could not be contained longer than a day and a half. The snipes may also have come from people whose theoretical persuasions were different from what I was presenting and who had to disqualify my presentation to support their own theories.

Ian's suggestion worked, probably for at least a couple of reasons. First, I was no longer anxious (and feeling out of control) because now I had my quirkiness to announce instead of waiting like a sitting duck to be sniped. Second, by prescribing the attack, I felt less helpless and vulnerable, since I was again in charge, and the snipers were less likely to snipe because I was requesting rather than fearing the snipe.

Since I have been using this prescription at workshops, I find that when there are questions after lunch on the second day, they are legitimate and lack the sniper-like edge that was associated with some questions from the audience before I prescribed the attack.

6

SOME FAVORITE RITUALS AND METAPHORS

SOME FAVORITE RITUALS

This chapter describes some of the therapeutic rituals and metaphors I have used with some degree of success in my private practice. Some rituals are general and may be used by other therapists for other situations. On the other hand, I am sure that there is always nonverbal information given by the family and used by the therapist in the formulation of rituals which by definition cannot easily be described. Further, the therapist's nonverbal expressions in "delivering" these rituals certainly contribute to their success. Unfortunately, it is not possible to completely capture these nonverbal messages in words. Despite these limitations, I usually have so much fun with these rituals that I thought I should share them with the reader. Even the patients and families enjoy some of these rituals after critical changes catalyzed by the ritual have taken place.

Antidote to the "I'll put my head in the oven" maneuver

This homework assignment is usually given to adults who are having trouble emotionally separating from their parents. I used it dramatically with a 50-year-old French professor who was about to go on his usual sabbatical to Paris. His

80-year-old mother was giving him messages that, if he went to Paris, she would probably not be around when he returned. The professor was quite upset about this and didn't know what to do.

The professor had initially entered treatment with his ex-wife to put some closure on their relationship. After some of this work was accomplished, the professor remained with me in treatment and began to share some of the problems he was having with his mother. The professor's father had died about five years earlier, and the mother was "being taken care of" by two of her older sisters. The sisters thought the mother was impossible because she refused medical care, medication, etc. The only person the mother listened to was her only son, the professor, my patient.

As the professor was preparing to go the Paris, his mother threatened to do herself in. When the professor was a child, mother would threaten to put her head in the oven and turn on the gas – and this was a very powerful way of influencing the professor during his earlier years. Naturally, with this kind of background, the professor was very concerned about what would happen to mother if he left for Paris.

I gave the professor the following homework: He was to take his mother out to dinner and at the appropriate moment tell her all the loving thoughts and feelings he has had for her, both presently and in the past. He was also to tell her in what ways she was a good mother to him. If mother asked why he was telling her all these loving, positive things, he was to say something like, "Well, Mother, it sounds like you are probably not going to be around when I return from Paris, and if that is the case, I wanted you to know how much I loved you, and I wanted to say these things to you before I no longer had the opportunity."

Upon hearing this the professor's mother told him that he was talking nonsense and that there would be lots of opportunities for him to say these things when he returned from Paris. The professor left for Paris with a clear conscience and found his mother alive and well in New York six months later when he returned.

I suspect the ritual worked because it placed the professor in a no-lose situation. Formerly he was placed in a no-win situation—if he went to Paris (which he wanted to do), his mother might commit suicide. If he stayed in New York to keep his mother alive, he couldn't be in Paris (which he would resent). The no-lose situation was created by telling mother all these loving things. If mother did herself in after he left for Paris, the professor knew that at least she died knowing about his love. If she didn't commit suicide after he left, he was still ahead, because he was able to tell her about his love for her— something all sons and daughters should do. Telling mother about his loving feelings would bring the two closer in a more adult relationship, a desirable goal.

One of the best victims I've seen in years

In doing psychotherapy for 15 years, one will naturally see many people who place themselves in victim positions. One reason why people enter therapy has to do with the pain they are experiencing, and often the pain has to do with their unwittingly placing themselves in victim positions, where they invite pain or are unable to protect themselves from painful situations they get themselves into with others. So I have seen a lot of victims (see Chapter 5) and witnessed how these victims get into painful situations.

What recently touched my little calloused heart and my funnybone at the same time was the case of 35-year-old recently-separated artist who was such a good boy and victim that he used to look for and buy only the dented cans in supermarkets. He felt sorry for the supermarket owner who was stuck with these cans and also didn't think himself deserving of undented cans. When he told me about the dented cans, I cracked up with laughter. He laughed a little, but not as much as I did.

This patient was referred to me because he had just broken up with his wife of one year after discovering that she was having an affair. The wife was seeing a colleague of mine, and when the husband indicated he wanted to see a therapist, my colleague referred him to me. During the first session, what stood out the most to me was how important it was for Fred to please others, to be liked, to be a nice guy, on one level, and how on a more covert level he felt deprived and furious about not getting what he wanted and needed. At the end of this first session I gave him one of my odd-even day rituals (Bergman, 1983b). On odd days he was to continue to be a nice guy, placing other people before himself, and basically act like a *shmatte* (pejorative Yiddish for rag, as in dishrag). On even days he was to begin doing more of what he wanted, provided it was legal and moral. At the end of the session, he asked me whether he should help his ex-wife-to-be pack her things that evening as he had previously promised. I told him that depended on how he felt and on whether the day was odd or even.

The next morning at 8 a.m., I received a call from my colleague (Fred's wife's therapist), who left a message on my answering machine asking what I had done to Fred, whose wife reported that Fred was "a new man." It happened that the wife kept postponing going to their apartment to pick up her things. What Fred did after the therapy session was throw all her makeup and clothing into the garbage (which was collected and removed by the New York City Department of Sanitation the following morning — unheard of efficiency!). Later he explained that he threw out all the deceptive coverings which made his wife appear different from her true self. The next day, when she found out about the clothing, the wife rushed over, afraid that he would next throw out her china, etc.

During the second session, Fred indicated that he felt terrific on even days and really enjoyed doing things he wanted to do rather than what he thought he should do. So much of therapy often consists of giving people permission to be themselves. In fact, he felt so good on even days that he continued to act the same way on odd days (he asked whether it was OK with me — still trying to be a good boy). During this second session, he went on to tell me how he felt victimized by his past. Fred shared with me that his uncle died on the day of his Bar Mitzvah, so no real celebration of his manhood could take place; that he once had a dream that he was responsible for all the suffering in the world; that his family was ashamed of him because he quit graduate school and became an artist rather than a doctor. He also had nightmares of being chased by Nazis.

At the end of the second session, I gave Fred the following ritual to do each morning for 15 minutes: He was to go down to the Lower East Side in New York and buy a *used* or *damaged* Bible, *talis*, and *yarmulke*. Each morning he was to face East, begin *davening* (rocking back and forth, holding the Bible and wearing the *yarmulke* and *talis*), and think only about all the suffering in the world and how he has personally contributed to this suffering. He was to do this ritual each morning. I set his next appointment for two weeks later.

Fred did the ritual and found it to be quite valuable. He no longer felt responsible for all the suffering in the world and asserted that it was no longer his destiny to take nonsense from people and always put others before himself. We ended the treatment after this fourth session.*

It takes at least two to tango

My mom is insecure and, like a good victim, never believes that she will get what she wants by being direct. So she sometimes makes things up. Because of my own great victim potential, I used to believe her and then become furious when I eventually discovered the truth.

One of my mom's favorite little white lies was her insistence that, despite Herculean efforts, she could never reach me by phone. When she finally contacted me, she would blast me and demand to know where I had been. I would defend myself, sheepishly telling her that I'd been busy.

One day she called to say that she had been unable to reach

---

*A training videotape of this case can be obtained from: IEA Productions, Inc., 520 East 77th St., Suite 132, New York, NY 10021.

me directly and had left a message on my telephone answering machine. Since there was no such message on the machine, I became upset because the machine is hooked up with my office phone, and if I hadn't gotten her call on the machine, I also might have missed patients' calls or new referrals. In addition, in my mind, if I miss calls from patients and referral contacts, I will lose my private practice and my autonomy, and become a dependent kid again—back in her clutches. Reactive and unthinking, I panicked and shipped my answering machine out for service. When the machine proved to be working fine, it dawned on me—my mother had set me up again and I had fallen for it.

A few months later she called and insisted again that she'd had a hard time reaching me by phone and had left a message on the answering machine. This time I told her, "I got your message on the machine [which she never left, and which I never received] and was just too busy this week to return your call. Please forgive me." My mother has since completely dropped her "I've been trying to reach you" dance.

Telling my mom that I received the message which she never left succeeded in getting me out of a victim position. By telling her that I received her nonexistent message, I confused her. I also metaphorically told her that I knew she was setting me up, without actually saying so. In the past, I had sometimes attacked her for lying. This always led to her denial and my feeling one-down. When I reversed course and told her that I received her message, her only way to recover was to say that she never left a message on the machine. But if she had said that, she would have had to admit that she was not telling the truth, which she would never do. Therefore, my statement forced her to stop setting me up.

This intervention effectively changed my position in this "I've been trying to reach you" dance. In the past I would be reactive, feel furious and victimized, and distance myself whenever I experienced the game. The intervention permitted me to be active, deal with the provocative dance differently, and still stay connected to my mom. So the intervention changed positions on both sides of the tango.

A memo to my brother

My brother is always asking me to do things with him and his wife. I love my brother and enjoy being with him when I'm with him, but he always appears to want more contact with me than I want with him. The more he persists, the more distance I create between us.

In the past he would typically call me and ask if I would like to do A, B, and C with him and his wife. These activities would usually involve things like mutual vacations or visits to resorts. I would look at my calendar, think about what I wanted to do, and then tell him that, although I couldn't make A and B, C sounded terrific. A few weeks or months later, he would call and ask why I hadn't sent him a deposit for A or B. When I replied that I had previously told him that I couldn't do A and B, he would deny it or say that I hadn't give him a "definite no." I would feel infuriated by this tactic, because I saw him as trying to disqualify me, my memory, and my wishes (a true victim position). I would also get angry realizing he was not telling the truth. If I confronted him on this, he (like my mother) would deny it.

Finally I decided it was time to change things. I went to the printer and had a memo pad printed with the following:

> "TO: MY BROTHER
> FROM: JOEL S. BERGMAN
> RE: CONFIRMATION OF LAST PHONE CON-
>   VERSATION."

I began sending a memo to his office following each phone discussion of some joint activity. Soon my brother stopped this dance.

This is what I think happened. My having the stationery printed suggested to my brother that I expected this problem of mine (his forgetfulness) to last for a long time. Rather than stay in control by lying, my brother may have been prompted by the specially printed stationery to stay in charge by telling the truth, since I expected him to lie for a long time. Printing the stationery also changed the covert game to an overt one. His receiving a confirmation memo of a phone conversation implied that I had retained a carbon copy, which he would have to eat when he experienced memory loss. The memo pad also implied that *he* had a memory problem and needed written confirmation. Finally, the memo system established that the less reliable my brother's memory (or the more he lied), the more he would be flooded with confirmations of past phone conversations. Faced with all this, my brother chose to have his memory problem cured, and I no longer feel victimized by him.

This intervention worked for me because, like the intervention used with my mom, it changed my position in the dance from being passive, reactive and angry to being active, dealing directly with the maneuver, and staying connected to my brother rather than distancing. Another possible consequence of this intervention is my recent realization that my brother "pins me down" by *appearing* to pursue me, when at times he might not even want to see me. Now I actively call him when I want to connect with him and quietly giggle to myself when he is busy, has other plans, etc. One more cat is out of the bag.

A ritual for an old maid

I was treating a couple who had been going with each other for a few years. She was 35 years old, and was placing great pressure on herself to get married. The more she pressured, the more the boyfriend resisted. Peggy was a social worker with good healthy California hysterical features, Alvin a psychologist with good healthy New York obsessive-compulsiveness – clearly, a marriage made in heaven.

Peggy was as ambivalent about marriage as Alvin, although she was the partner who was responsible for pressing the couple to make more of a commitment to the relationship. Whenever she made a move towards more of a commitment, they would break up. Then they would miss each other and get back together. Then they would break up again, etc.

At one point Peggy requested an individual session, a request I honored since I thought it would be helpful. During this session, she shared with me her basic terror of never getting married, never having a family, never leading a normal life, and winding up an old maid.

Recently she had become increasingly obsessed about the new wrinkles which she observed on her face and the appearance of more and more grey hair. At the end of the session, I gave Peggy the following ritual: Every other evening she was to dress up like an old spinster – wear a black dress, put a pillow under her dress to make her appear plump, place her hair in a bun, use a cane, walk with a slight limp, hunch her back – so she could begin to feel what it will be like to be an old maid. She was to do this every other evening after coming home from work. I scheduled her next appointment in two weeks.

At the next session, Peggy reported doing the ritual very conscientiously. In fact, after a few days she got into the whole scene. An important thing happened each time Peggy went out walking as an old maid – she experienced an irresistible impulse to skip or hop. This lead to the realization that her insides would always be young and playful, and she didn't have to worry so much about the rest. More importantly, she relaxed about the marital commitment, and soon thereafter Alvin proposed to her. A few months later, I received a note from Peggy telling me of their marriage, the ceremony, and how important that ritual was for her. She signed the note, "Sadie, married lady!"

"Have another drink, dear!"

I use this ritual whenever the therapy seems to be frozen in a certain way. The freeze consists of one partner's being obsessed and blaming of the other partner, who is involved in some variety of substance abuse. As long as treatment remains focused on this interaction, very little progress can be made toward change.

I explain to the couple that the substance abuser is absorbing the tension which exists in the relationship and that he or she should be thanked rather than blamed. I then tell the non-drug-abusing partner that the next time she gets anxious, she should offer the abusing partner a drink, joint, snort, or whatever the abuse happens to be.

I treated a couple whose focus was entirely on the husband's drinking. The partners had known each other for 15 years and had been married for 11 years. The ritual I prescribed was the following: The wife was told to offer the husband a drink whenever she felt anxious or was getting too close to her husband. Husband was to graciously receive the drink, face South (where the wife's mother lived — it was established earlier in the session that the wife was still very attached to her mother) and toast the wife's mother by saying, "Rest assured, Mrs. S., that your daughter still loves you more than anyone else."

At the next session, the couple came in fighting like hell, and treatment was no longer focused on the drinking. He stopped drinking by the second day after the session, and the overt fighting began. This is exactly where I wanted the couple to be, and I could begin working on the marital issues, which were no longer frozen or camouflaged as a drinking problem.

Shopping lists and orgasms

During a marital therapy session, the wife complained about how unsatisfactory things were in the love-making department. The husband confirmed this difficulty and quietly complained (very much like Woody Allen) that he sometimes fears lockjaw while he is trying to stimulate his wife. Further inquiry revealed that while they are making love, the wife's mind drifts, and she begins to obsess, ruminate, worry about things, and make shopping lists — basically, she goes elsewhere.

I suggested to the couple that the wife's mind possibly goes elsewhere in loyalty to her widowed mother, who lives alone in Chicago. As a consequence of some of their work in treatment, the wife was feeling closer to the husband in other ways, and if she got closer to him in the last remaining way, she might fear that her mother would feel endangered. The wife did not believe this was the case.

I then instructed the husband to find a picture of the wife's mother, have it enlarged professionally to poster size, and attach it to the ceiling over the wife's side of the bed. Then, if the wife was going to be loyal to her mother, she wouldn't have to do it half-heartedly by thinking of shopping lists. Instead, she could formally and overtly give her mother the loyalty that this daughter feels towards her mother.

At the next session, the couple revealed that they did not place a picture over the wife's side of the bed. They also reported that the wife has mysteriously become much more relaxed and responsive in the love-making department.

"I had a dream"

A 50-year-old woman came to see me after being referred by her older sister, a family therapist whom I may have met briefly but do not really know.

A brief history revealed that the patient had recently broken up with her 40-year-old boyfriend with whom she had lived for eight years. She had been married before that but got divorced after 10 years; she has two children in their early twenties who are off on their own; and she still receives alimony from her ex-husband. She is the managing editor of a magazine she thinks will soon fold; she works for a very self-centered boss for whom she has little respect.

Recently she was asked by the editor of a prestigious magazine to write a feature article on women. In the patient's mind, if she were able to write this piece, it would provide her with the confidence, money and opportunity to move to California, live on a farm with a friend, and write for a living — something she has always dreamed of doing. Instead, she recently called this editor and told her that she would be unable to write the feature. In addition to her tale of woe, the patient also told me that she has been in individual treatment for 15 years but had stopped seeing her former therapist because he knew her too well and they were now more like friends than doctor and patient.

This is the ritual I presented to this depressed, lonely woman: I told her that she must call her older sister (who referred her to me), her ex-boyfriend, her ex-husband, and her boss. She was to tell each of them of a nightmare she had the night before. The nightmare was that she became a famous writer — but that she was haunted by this fear that the more famous, celebrated and rich she became from writing, the more her sister (ex-boyfriend, ex-husband, boss) would be endangered. Then I told the patient to carefully pay attention to the nonverbal (emotional, vocal) behaviors of the person to whom she was telling her nightmare. I suggested that the quality of the nonverbal reactions to her reported nightmare would tell her whom she was protecting.

I then went on vacation, so the jury is out on the ritual. I did get a check in the mail and note from the patient saying "Even though I'm not cured, you did give me a lot to think about. So if I ever get over my writing block, I'm going to write an article on brief therapy and call it 'Fast Food for Thought.' Or maybe I'll review your book. Happy Summer."

Pick on food rather than on children

A family was referred to me by a colleague who could not make any progress with them. The family had a history of defeating psychotherapists.

The presenting problem was the second child, Chris, age 10, who had been in psychotherapy since the age of five, and who was now having school problems which were behavioral rather than academic. He would "twirl, make disgusting faces and sounds, and sometimes would take out and wear the *au pair's* underwear."

Chris was the second of two adopted sons; the oldest was Daniel, age 12. In addition, this family had two biological children, aged three years and 18 months. So there were two families — an earlier family with two adopted sons, and a later one with a biological son and daughter. Chris and Daniel were placed in therapy at ages five and four, respectively. When, while taking a history and doing a genogram, I learn of sticking kids into therapy so early in life, I have many reactions. My first reaction is anger – how can these parents do this to kids so young? My second reaction is to see the parents as abdicating their roles as parents. The third reaction is a suspicion that the parents are using psychotherapists as the benevolent parents (and for their kids, grandparents) that the parents never experienced. The fourth is a hypothesis that obtaining a history from the parents will document that these parents had very little good parenting.*

In this case both parents lacked good mothering – mother's mother was described as a "socialite," and father's mother a "space cadet." There was some tenderness and nurturing shown by the fathers on both sides.

It has been my experience that one way in which unparented parents can obtain parenting is to purchase it under the respectable umbrella of psychotherapy. Father and mother also averaged around 12 years each in individual psychotherapy.

Because of the history of resistance to therapy in this family, I ended the first session by prescribing the identified patient's symptoms. The dynamics of this family were very clear in the sense that the marital battles were fought through the kids; father used Chris as the scapegoat and mother protected Chris, whereas mother used Daniel as the scapegoat, and father protected Daniel. As expected, very little fighting went on between the two parents. I also told Chris that if he could not protect his parents with his distractions or if he got too tired, he should get Daniel to help him out.

---

*One of the problems for families and therapists when this situation occurs is that the parents have to give up their good therapist parents when the children are no longer symptomatic. This was a problem for me when I was treating an impossible 14-year-old who had been in psychotherapy since she was four years old. The parents became so close with the child's therapist that the therapist became part of the family – and the inherent danger involved in this family was that the family treatment would cure the child and the parents would then have to give up this wonderful, benevolent child therapist and would find this unbearable. So the child had to remain symptomatic so the family would not risk losing the child therapist.

When the family returned two weeks later, the parents were no longer focused on Chris; rather, they were completely focused on Daniel. I congratulated the two sons on fulfilling the therapy homework assigned to them. In addition, the enormous parental differences on parenting became quite evident during this session. There was not one thing the parents agreed upon. This is, of course, the marital differences coming out as parenting differences. To point this out to parents when the symptoms involve children is tempting, but a mistake because the *parents* are focused on the child and not on the marriage, and because there are good reasons why the parents are focused on the child and not them – this has to be respected. We ended the session by giving the family two small, circumscribed behavioral goals to agree and act upon with the children – one having to do with getting up from the dinner table, the other having to do with the children's behavior while traveling in cars.

The next session included just the parents, because Daniel was going to summer camp and I didn't want Chris there without Daniel. This was a dangerous move because: 1) the parents were still focused on the children's symptom; 2) they were not asking for couple therapy, and their overt differences were over parenting rather than coupling; 3) the parents were likely to remain totally focused on the children and not on themselves.

This is exactly what happened. I am not exactly sure about how the next sequence of events occurred, but the session shifted to talk about being overweight, deprived, oral, etc. Father is 80 pounds overweight and mother 30 pounds overweight. I had just gained 15 pounds myself over a two-month period since I quit smoking cigarettes. It turns out that father was as skinny as a rail when he married. So it seemed that the couple needed an 80-pound space between the two, a few symptomatic kids, and a few psychotherapists to maintain some balance in the family.

At the end of the session, I told father that whenever he was inclined to scapegoat, overreact and become "too harsh" (mother's words) to Chris, he was to go to the kitchen and eat something. We all laughed at the prescription.

At the next session, two weeks later, Chris was doing even better and there was no anxiety in session about the children. Both children were away in summer camp. Nor was there any anxiety about the marriage or marital conflict, which I usually expect when the children's symptoms are eliminated. Father did not scapegoat or overreact to Chris *nor* did he go to kitchen to eat something if he had such impulses. We ended the therapy with the usual invitation to call me in the event something comes up.

For me, the interesting thing about this case was that we never touched the marriage. Somehow the couple dealt with this by themselves. The curious thing about this couple was how boring they were. I kept on yawning through the session, my videoperson kept yawning, and my students at Ackerman to whom I showed this tape kept reacting to the boredom. I think that maybe one of the ways I won this couple over was by trying to be kindly towards their boring souls, and trying to be interested in them. I'm not sure what the boredom was about, and whether it was a powerful controlling part of the therapy. I'm also not sure whether there was a real shift or a temporary shift in this family, and whether the family will come back or not.

The other curious thing about this case was that father repeatedly asked me how Dr. X (a well-known male family therapist) was doing. Father had been in treatment with Dr. X, liked him a lot, and wondered how he was doing after he returned from a foreign country. I tried to update father on Dr. X as best as I could. Somehow I think father was metaphorically telling me that men or male therapists stabilize his family's system, perhaps by bearing symptoms or by being therapists. I don't know but it seems to have something to do with stabilization. We will see.

"Honey, it's time for your rage practice"

I was treating a couple where most of the overt symptomatology was being carried by the husband. He was considerably overweight and was sexually disinterested in his wife. He was also quite furious with his wife and collected hundreds of little unexpressed hurts and slights. He was unable to express this anger, except indirectly in terms of overeating and refusing to have sex with his wife. There were some primary reasons why the anger could not directly be expressed: First, the husband came from a family in which verbalizing anger was discouraged; second, he and his wife had made some sort of covert deal to protect the wife – it's hard to protect someone and be angry at her at the same time.

The wife, on the other hand, had little trouble being verbally critical of husband. When she criticized him, he would take it in and quietly fume. When I told the wife during one treatment session that the more she criticized husband the less likely it was that the couple would have sex (she was sexy and liked sex), this did not seem to help.

Finally, I gave the couple a homework assignment. He was to practice verbally expressing anger on even days of the week and she was to help him with this homework by making outrageous requests of him and being critical of him for outrageous things. On odd days, wife was to resume her natural schedule of being critical of husband for real and unoutrageous things.

The husband found the homework very helpful. When wife started being critical, he immediately looked at his calendar watch to see if the day was odd or even. If it was even, he knew it was a game (that's how terrified he was of the wife's anger). Once he knew it was a game, he could begin expressing some of his anger in these little fights; in fact he learned that he could express some of his anger without letting go of his murderous rage, which he thought would kill his wife. This was the first step in learning how to fight with his spouse.

The homework had an interesting paradoxical effect on the wife's criticism. In effect, the wife reduced her criticism on *both* odd and even days. It was hard for her to come up with outrageous requests (perhaps because it was on my terms rather than hers), and it was hard for her to come up with real criticisms (perhaps for the same reason). Nevertheless, with the husband verbally showing more normal anger and the wife showing less criticism on both days, the marital dance shifted. More sex occurred in the relationship and the husband seemed to feel powerful. A few weeks later, the wife was grandstanding, threatening not to go to some social affair which was important to the husband, and the husband went without her. To his great surprise and joy, he had a terrific time. The wife was surprised that he went without her, and admitted that recently she has felt less of a need to do grandstanding with her husband.

Rituals for "helpless people"

Frequently therapists encounter patients and couples who play helpless and want the therapist to decide things for them. Most patients know that therapists will not make important decisions for them, and often telling them this directly and indirectly is sufficient. However, when patients persist in trying to get the therapist to decide for them questions such as, "Should I get an abortion?" "Should I marry her?" "Should I quit my job?" "What private school should the kids go to?" etc., there are a few things the therapist can do, if he or she has a sense of humor and playfulness.

1) When an unmarried pregnant woman persisted in asking me to decided whether she should have an abortion or not, I eventually took out a coin and asked her whether she was calling heads or tails.
2) I enjoy telling patients to take a poll, to ask neighbors, strangers, or family members what they should do.
3) I suggest that the patient look at the daily lottery number; if it is odd he should marry the gal, and if even, not. The answer to the problem must be as absurd as the question.

Any dramatic example of arbitrariness will do. The more dramatic the better. The more arbitrary the better. The more dramatic and arbitrary, the more the response is powerful and absurd, the less likely the patient will persist in pushing the therapist to decide for him or her. It also gives the patient the message that while he vacillates his fate might be dictated by something random. That might mobilize him toward some decision.

A penny for your problems

In 1976, I went to a training workshop with Dick Fisch at the Center for Family Learning in New Rochelle. At the end of the live interview, he instructed the father to go up to the symptomatic girl each time she was symptomatic and give her a penny, without saying a word. Then he was to carry on with what he was doing.

I was impressed by the simplicity and elegance of the intervention and how much it captured a complicated family situation. In a way, the intervention can be seen as a prototype intervention to use whenever a child's symptom is balancing some marital struggle. In the family situation to which Fisch consulted, the child was verbally abusing mother and mother seemed to tolerate the abuse (all powerful children sit on the shoulders of one parent). As one could imagine, father had difficulty expressing his anger towards his wife, so little daughter did his work. The task of father giving daughter a penny each time she does his work is an example of making the covert overt. This changes the game and often leads to disappearance of the symptom.

One of my favorite variations of this ritual is to ask parents to formally thank the identified patient for being symptomatic. Saying "thank you" is often so toxic to the parents that they eventually kick the symptomatic kid out of their marriage and begin to take some responsibility for their marital conflict and its resolution.

Prescribing exaggerations as
a learning device

A wife complained bitterly about her husband's arrogant, omniscient, holier-than-thou way of responding to her and their daughter. Daughter agreed that this was Dad's style.

The father, a family therapist, was floored that he was seen that way, and could not understand where his two women got this impression.

The homework assignment I gave to father was that whenever he was giving orders and coming off as omniscient he was to be given "two tablets" by wife or daughter and told to do "Moses coming down from Mt. Sinai." I had a feeling, since this guy reminded me of myself, that he wouldn't learn anything from taking "humility lessons." That would be too humiliating. However, exaggerating Moses coming down from Mt. Sinai would be closer, easier, and more interesting.

Anyway, the whole family got into it. The husband even got a staff with which he now walks around. The ritual was helpful to the husband. However, at the next session, he revealed that his back went completely out, and now he is dependent upon his daughter and wife—which was also a blessing, since Moses never knew how to ask for things or be helpless. It could also be that this husband needs to always be in charge, and his two extreme positions are either Moses or Jesus Christ. This case is still in progress, so we'll see what develops over time.

An undoing ritual for marital resentment

When a couple comes in for treatment, quite often the therapist finds considerable resentment in one or both partners. The resentment may be the end-result of unexpressed hurt and anger accumulated over many years. Sometimes the resentment is consciously experienced by one or both partners so that it can be *verbally* expressed to both the other partner and the therapist. Other times, the partner is unaware of the resentment. Such unexpressed and/or unacknowledged resentment can become manifest in other behavioral forms, not only producing second-order couple problems, but also interfering with the couple treatment.

For example, it is not uncommon to find a couple seeking treatment where the husband is furious about accumulated and carefully nurtured past hurts. (Of course, the reverse also occurs where the wife is the accumulator of unexpressed fury.) His anger has never been *directly* and *verbally* expressed to the wife; in fact, sometimes the husband isn't even aware of the fury or doesn't know that it is appropriate to feel or express his anger. The husband may not express his anger for a variety of reasons. Maybe the wife *appears* fragile, or perhaps he came from a family where there were sanctions against expressing anger, or he may simply believe, as some boys are taught early in life, that he should not fight with girls.

So what does the husband do with this accumulation of unexpressed hurt and anger? Husbands do many things, such as become passive, withdraw, get depressed, or use what I call "passive-aggressive guerrilla-war tactics." The wife then reacts to the husband's secondary responses to his anger, and the couple then escalates to produce the state the couple is in when they seek treatment. The husband's attempt to deal with his hurt and anger with withdrawal or passive-aggressive guerrilla-war tactics is a solution which becomes the problem. Thus, new ways must be found for the husband to deal with his hurt and anger in a way which works for the couple.

Often, the therapist does not become aware of this fury in the first session because it is not verbalized or shown nonverbally by the partners, who are focused on other issues. However, in the *second* session the therapist becomes aware of the fury when he learns that the couple did not do the homework assignment given to them at the end of the first session. And sometimes the homework was not done because one or both marital partners are so furious. Obviously, if a therapist is going to work strategically with the couple, then he must attempt to eliminate the resentment.

The ritual described below has been helpful to couples who are still quite connected to each other and consciously want to keep their relationship from breaking up. The ritual reduces the resentment, permitting the couple to act on subsequent homework assignments.

In some couples, the hurt and fury are so overwhelming that the couple has great difficulty even initiating this homework ritual. This inability gives the therapist important information about the couple. For example, one of the resentful partners may be unwilling to give up his or her victim position in the relationship, and is therefore unwilling to initiate this ritual. Some professional victims are so accustomed to seeing their world from a one-down position that they become terrified of what life would be like from a different position. Consequently, it may be important to know how readily the partners are willing to give up victim positions. When one finds intractable victims, one then gets important information which might temporarily change the goals of treatment. For example, the spouses may not really be interested in getting together or being content; rather, they may be looking for an outside witness to acknowledge how much suffering one or both are experiencing. The therapist learning about this would immediately stop his or her efforts to bring them together (or apart) or to reduce the pain; instead he might volunteer to be an impartial judge who may be willing to determine who is suffering the best in each session.

This is the way the ritual works. Usually, I see couples every other week for an hour to an hour and a half and assign homework at the end of each session. I have found through experimentation that a two-week interval between sessions appears optimal for the couples to do homework assignments and for the homework ritual to begin to take effect in changing the relationship.

When I sense unspoken resentment or when the homework assignment is not done after the first session, I give the couple the following *undoing ritual.*

Every evening (for the next two weeks), the couple is to find a private place where there will be no distractions or interruptions. For the first five minutes, one partner (usually the overtly resentful one), whom we will call partner A, will tell partner B the ways in which A was hurt by B in the past. Partner A will take an "I" position and enumerate, in an unangry, non-blaming way, how and when A's feelings have been hurt by B. Partner B is to quietly listen, not responding until A's laundry list has been completed. At the end of A's five-minute statement, B is to recite the following: "I have been unaware and sorry about the ways you have felt hurt and hope that some day you will forgive me." Following B's statement, B is to tell A for the next five minutes the ways in which B has felt hurt by A, and after B's laundry list has been shared, A is to say "I have been unaware and sorry about the ways you have felt hurt and hope that some day you will forgive me."

This ritual does several things. First, it requires that the partners take "I" positions and begin verbalizing internal reactions and statements to one another. Some couples need permission to express their insides to others.

Second, when partners are required to express themselves in "I" positions, they begin to learn that *they* must be responsible for what happens to them. The process of using "I" positions and speaking up for themselves begins to help them get out of victim positions. In addition, this always involves an implied reduction in the amount of blaming and name-calling in the relationship. One thing I do in treatment is forbid blaming and name-calling. I explain to couples that hurt precedes anger, and anger precedes attack and blame. It thus become incumbent on both partners to practice verbalizing their hurt and anger before the anger sours into blame and attack. I continue by pointing out that once hurt has turned to anger and then to blame and attack, the receiving partner immediately shuts down and becomes deaf to the attacker's complaints. When there is considerable resistance to not attacking, I point out to the resistant spouse that the best way to make sure that he or she will not be heard is to blame and attack. If this doesn't work, I might suggest to the attacker that he is simply replicating the ways in which his parents treated him – and he knows how invalidating and painful those experiences were for him in the past.

Third, by having each partner share his or her laundry list of past hurts over a two-week period, the ritual conveys important information to the partner: a) Each partner learns how his/her behavior has affected and hurt the other partner; b) people who have storage banks of past hurts have the op-

portunity and time to begin "unloading"; c) partners learn
that they can verbalize their hurts, learn about how they have
participated in that hurt, talk with one another about it, and
forgive.

Quite often, partners are surprised about which of their behaviors have hurt or offended the other partner. So there is
also an information-sharing situation, where learning about
the other partner's sensitivities occurs. I may have the spouses
write down their lists of hurts and bring the lists to the next
session. These lists provide a wealth of material for subsequent sessions. If partners are able to make up their lists of
hurts, but are unable to act upon the forgiving ritual, I will
then have them do the ritual at the next session, where things
are somewhat safer. As the couple performs the ritual in the
session, I will actively coach each partner in speaking up and
sharing their insides, using an "I" position. Spouses do need
to practice thinking and verbalizing in "I" position, since there
appears to be a very strong tendency for most "untrained"
people to attack others whom they see as hurtful towards
them. Even the author, who has been teaching patients to use
"I" positions for years, will sometimes slip and go into an attack. So it takes practice, and patients should be told this.

Fourth, the ritual gives the couple an opportunity to see
the benefits of touching down with each other and suggests
that a forum is needed in the relationship for the two to sit
down and talk.

There are many benefits to this ritual, and different
couples take to different parts of it and use what they consider helpful to them. For the therapist, it is a powerful, concrete ritual to begin the "thawing-out process" needed to work
with resentful couples.

*"When you really need the money,
you can count on us!"*

In some families there exists a myth, passed on from parent to child, that "when you (the child) really need the money,
you can count on us (the parents)." This is often a loving state-

ment from parents to children where helping out the children usually refers to financially helping out with a down payment towards a house, although the money may be spent differently. Variations on this include "When you really need us, we will be there," and, of course, "blood is thicker than water."

Now this kind of helping has been going on for centuries. And as far as I am concerned there is nothing wrong with it, as long as it is helping out and not maintaining a prolonged dependency, which some of my adult patients seem to experience with their parents. Parents in their fifties and sixties often do have more money than their children in their twenties and thirties, and helping out or lending money to grown children is not unusual. However, things get tricky when there are strings associated with the money and when parents don't mean what they say.

For instance, parents might lend some money towards a house, but then see themselves as a major stockholders or investors in the house. In certain families, it may be hard for parents to *not* see themselves as major stockholders. In such fused families, the children may go along with the major stockholders for various reasons. Children in less fused families may recognize that it would be "cleaner" and certainly more grownup to pay a few percentage points more and get the mortgage from a bank. Then, the couple, rather than the bank or the parents, could decide on the color of the kitchen, bathroom tile, etc. What is saved borrowing from the parents when the price paid is remaining a child to these parents?

One of the interesting things about the statement, "when you need the money, you can count on us," is how it can freeze the ongoing relationship between the potential lender and lendee. In certain families, there are hidden provisions or conditions on how the child is supposed to be or act in order to qualify for this help when he or she needs it. Another interesting thing about this "gift" is that it is given in the unknown future in a situation which may or may not ever develop.

This myth played a role in a recent case. Stan and Barbara, a couple in their early thirties, had been

married for a few years. Stan was an artist whose
wealthy mother encouraged his art and acted as his
patron. His father was a millionaire in his own right,
who was divorced from Stan's mother and remarried.
Father always wanted his son to work for him in the
family business. So one can see how Stan was split
between mother's and father's aspirations.

Since their marriage Barbara had been supporting
Stan by working as a TV producer. Barbara, like
mother, wanted Stan to paint, but was tired of working and, since she was getting into her thirties, wanted to start a family. The couple had been trying for
two years to conceive a child without success. Stan
was clearly in a bind between his benefactor mother
and his wife. If he stayed dependent upon his benefactor, he would not earn enough money to have a family, and if he went out and worked for a living at a "real
job," he would paint less, and disappoint his mother.

Both parents had promised Stan that whenever he
needed money, it would be there. In addition, he had
been told that there were "trusts" in his name which
he could also draw upon in the event he needed money.

The drama unfolded when he finally went to both
parents, saying that he needed the money because,
although he still wanted to paint, he also wanted to
start a family. For the first time, Stan looked into
these trusts to see how much money was available.
His father told him that the money was not liquid and
that a great deal of money would be lost if he made
it liquid now. From mother came the message that
she would gladly give him a certain amount of money
either outright or on a monthly basis. Mother then
indicated that, incidentally, she would love to start
a small business with Stan and Barbara.

When he asked for the money, rather than leaving
the myth untested, Stan found that the money was
not really there or had strings attached. He went
through some feelings of disappointment, hurt and

anger. Following this experience, he was able to get on with his life as an adult, rather than remain a child and wait around until the money was there. Stan subsequently made some decisions about how he was going to paint *and* support a family, and a few months later, Barbara became pregnant.

I think forcing the myth, or uncovering the myth, may hasten the differentiation process for certain individuals from fused families. The issue is tricky, because I do not mean to suggest that people go out and buy houses or start families *just* to see if their parents mean what they say. But I do recommend that children of such "supportive" parents reasonably test the notion that "when you really need the money, you can count on us." When this is indeed a myth, and it is uncovered, considerable growing-up and emotional separation are possible on both the parents' and children's side.

How to avoid being controlled by someone else's need for closeness

One of the most dramatic demonstrations of systems theory occurs to me when I am treating someone who is complaining that he or she is feeling controlled by another person's need for closeness. The typical scenario involves a patient, "John," and his girlfriend, "Mary."

Now the problem which John mentions to me in treatment is that Mary is always pursuing John, looking for more closeness and affection, and that's fine with John up to a point. Then John begins to distance from Mary, Mary further pursues John, John distances further but also feels guilty about this because it *appears* that Mary is not being that unreasonable. Therefore, in John's mind, there must be something wrong with him because he cannot handle this closeness.

In such situations, I point out to John that the couple at this particular moment is involved in a tango where John is in charge of distance and Mary is in charge of closeness in the relationship. I further emphasize that John is in charge of distance for *both* John and Mary. If John wants to stop feeling guilty about distancing from Mary, he just has to give Mary the closeness she seeks or "reverse engines" and pursue Mary for closeness rather than be in charge of the distance.

Usually, at the next session, I get a delighted report from John about how startled he was when he pursued Mary and she started distancing. John then takes charge of space and closeness for himself, leaving Mary to be more responsible for her own space and closeness. It is also a good experience for John to stop feeling helpless, pathological, and defensive about distancing—since he now understands this more as a systems phenomenon, and he can always reduce feeling badly about distancing by pursuing Mary and having Mary do some of the distancing.

Buying term life insurance
for loved ones

Sometimes in the middle of couple treatment, one partner starts showing concern about the self-destructive behavior of the spouse. A husband may become concerned about his wife's drinking, or a wife may become focused on her husband's eating and smoking habits following his second heart attack.

These abuses must first be investigated to see how they are systematically related to the marital relationship. For example, the abuse might be absorbing tension for the couple (see "Have another drink, dear!" in this chapter).

All therapists know how difficult it is to change eating and smoking habits, particularly when the change is sought by the non-abusing partner. When the excessive eating or smoking does not seem to be systematically related (and I suspect that sometimes it's not), I suggest another intervention.

For example, if the wife is concerned about the husband's weight, his smoking and his heart condition, there really is not much the wife can do—since the needed changes must come from the husband. To give the wife something concrete to do (and at the same time convey a metaphorical message to the husband), I suggest that the wife begin to buy as much term life insurance on her husband as she can, and begin to start looking at other men.

At first, the spouses laugh since they think I am being a smart ass. When they realize I am serious, the wife begins to get into it—she is no longer helpless about her husband. Sometimes this intervention helps the husband change some of his habits. More importantly, it gets the wife out of this helpless complaining position—and she either does something or stops complaining.

Terminating treatment as an intervention

While we are on the subject of termination, I would like to describe yet another therapeutic posture I sometimes take which I call "termination of treatment as an intervention."

My tennis partner, a psychologist, was complaining to me one day how a bulimic patient he was seeing in individual treatment was making him anxious and forcing him to jump over all kinds of hurdles. He was presently worried about some medical condition of hers, but she refused to go to a physician to check it out. As I finished tying my sneakers in the locker room, I told my partner to tell this patient that if she didn't check out this condition with a physician, he would be forced to terminate treatment with her.

My partner liked the idea of using treatment termination as leverage, and it worked. I think all therapists should feel comfortable knowing that they can terminate treatment whenever the treatment conditions get to a point where the therapist can no longer do therapy.

A similar situation happened to me when I was seeing an individual patient who began talking about suicide. The moment I heard this, I asked the patient to give me a list of ten family members and their telephone numbers, so I could contact them to place the family on suicide watch (see Chapter 7). The patient at first refused to give me this information, so I told her that she was terminating treatment, because I could not work under such conditions.

We left it at that, and I said "goodbye" to the patient. One week later, I received the names and phone numbers of the family members by mail, with an apology from the patient about how she behaved. The patient now knows that the next time she mentions suicide her family will be contacted and a suicide watch will be initiated.

When a therapist gets into a situation where he or she has to work with a "gun to his head" he cannot work anyway, so using termination as an intervention to change the therapeutic conditions makes enormous sense. A suicide maneuver puts the patient or family in charge, and termination as an intervention puts the therapist back in charge. As I have emphasized elsewhere, when the patient is in charge, very little treatment takes place.

SOME FAVORITE METAPHORS

I like using metaphors. I find them to be powerful, colorful, dramatic, and three-dimensional. They are also poetic and musical. They grab the mind more than non-metaphorical expressions. Since I see symptoms as metaphors, I like to use therapeutic metaphors to counter the symptom as metaphor. Here are some of my favorites.

Radar

I use the term "radar" often, particularly when I am making reference to how the identified patient becomes symptomatic to protect someone else in the family. I tell the family that the patient has radar.

Radar is a convenient and accurate metaphor because radar cannot be seen or heard. It tracks and focuses on signals close and far away, and it does so accurately and silently. When parents claim the identified patient has been living in California and is hardly in contact with the family, I just make my statements about radar and usually the identified patient beams (radar, of course).

Submarines

I use this term to refer to people who take huge one-down positions with respect to someone else. I contrast submarines with tanks (see below) who are people who take powerful one-up positions with respect to somebody else. Submarines, of course, are more lethal than tanks because they cannot be seen until there is a torpedo coming right at you, and then it is too late. A submarine would be, for example, a person who enters a room and asks you whether it is OK with you if he shares some of the air in the room, or a person who orders a radish sandwich when you take him out to lunch — because he was so poor growing up that he wouldn't know how to eat something more extravagant, like a cheese sandwich. When I see someone in the act of being a submarine, I start saying to myself (and sometimes out loud) "Dive! Dive! Dive!" — the way submarines use to dive in World War II pictures.

Tanks

Tanks are powerful, usually noisy, bulldozer-type people, who go straight for what they want and may trample you in the process. They are tactless people, who forget that there are others out there with feelings which may be different from their own. Tanks, of course, have cannons and can be dangerous. However, because they are slow and noisy, they are detectable and vulnerable, particularly to submarines (see above). When I was a kid, growing up in my family, I saw my mother as a tank, my father a submarine. Believe me, submarines are more powerful. Tanks are often noisy because they are so powerless compared with submarines.

Hummingbird talk

I never knew about this way of talking until I became a professor at a prestigious women's college in New England. From departmental meetings and faculty-parent teas, I learned about hummingbird talk. Hummingbird talk is basically talk-

ing with someone for a half-hour and saying nothing. I liken
it to a hummingbird which can stay suspended and almost
motionless over a flower for an endless period of time — ex-
pending enormous energy and showing no movement.

Kissy kissy talk

This derives more from the metropolitan New York area
than from prep schools in New England. Basically it describes
the way individuals who cannot tolerate any negativity or
pain in their consciousness, and the way they talk to others
(and perhaps themselves). It is a phony, superficial posture,
that life is terrific, wonderful, and one is having a ball at all
times. Unlike victims (whose *raison d'être* is pain and the advertisement of pain), kissy kissy people avoid dealing with
any pain at all. They are good candidates for addictions (food,
drug, alcohol, TV, gambling, sex).

Leave it to your sister-in-law

Good victims know how to work hard, but have little or
no sense of how to play or how to spend money on themselves. Part of being a victim is seeing oneself as working
very hard and getting nothing in return. Victims get nothing
in return because they don't know about fun and relaxation
and because they don't take care of themselves. If they did,
they would be less furious and feel less victimized. So, one
of the things I do with victims in therapy is "force them" to
take better care of themselves (by spending money on what
they want and need). Believe it or not, with professional victims this is hard to do. One of the ways I help victims learn
to spend money on themselves is to point out to them that
they are working so hard, and having so little fun, in part because they don't spend money on pleasurable activities, that
they are going to drop dead soon from their life schedule and
their sister-in-law will probably benefit the most. I use sister-
in-law (or brother-in-law) because it usually is the most toxic
to the patient. Some patients might not resent blood relatives

(like parents or sibs) inheriting money from them after they die, but usually in fused families, out-laws are resented the most because they remain strangers.

Marrying garlic

One way to get out of your fused, undifferentiated family (if you plan not to work on your family of origin with a qualified family therapist) is to "marry garlic." That is, you should choose someone so disgusting and offensive that you never have to learn how to decline invitations for dinner or family gatherings because your parents and sibs are so offended by the garlic you married that they do not invite you.

Marrying kosher garlic

A subtle variation of marrying garlic is seen in some of the young couples I have treated from the New York area. What one does is go to Israel (for a junior year abroad, or over the summer, or for a year to "find oneself") and return to New York married to another young Jewish New Yorker who went to Israel for similar reasons. The kicker here is that the newly married spouses are now extremely observant Orthodox Jews. Now, instead of offending mother by saying you don't want to come for dinner on Fridays because, "It's boring, offensive, and I hate chicken," you can say, "We'd love to come but, as you know, we must be home before sunset." To those unfamiliar with Jewish law, it is important to point out that Jewish law and holidays are so extensive that you can find wonderful excuses for not visiting parents at all. In addition, if you can't use the law and holidays, you can use the excuse of having to travel an extra 80 miles that day to get kosher milk for the baby. What grandparents could refuse kosher milk for their grandchild?

The elegance of this maneuver is that it is impossible for the parents to object to their children's taking the Jewish religion more seriously than they do. These parents probably emphasized the importance of religious traditions to their children when they were youngsters. Well, as the commercial says, "You asked for it—you got it."

Barracuda

Barracuda are, of course, killer families that eat therapists. They can be detected by the smiles on their faces and the glee in their voices when they describe the chronicity of their problem and the list of therapists they have devoured. The name of this game is not therapy, but "let's get some new therapists to munch on for some nutritional homeostasis."

High rollers and big gamblers

These terms are the Italian translations of barracuda (Palazzoli et al., 1977). They refer to the extreme positions and escalations family members take to stay in charge of the family system. Anorexia, bulimia, schizophrenia, murder, homicide—are all examples of *positions* people take to maintain control or homeostasis in the family system. Here, of course, is the paradox—that people are willing to die to stay in charge.

Good-boy and good-girl heaven

These are expressions I use to tease some of my patients out of the need for approval from others, which invariably gets in their way of growing up, taking charge of their lives, and having some fun. If they are complaining about the price they are paying because of their incessant need for approval, I remind them that their suffering will not go unheeded because they are accumulating points in good-boy or good-girl heaven. My comments are sometimes sufficiently infuriating to get the patients to start doing things for themselves.

Running 220 voltage through a 110 line

This is a metaphor I use when a marital partner is trying to get from a marriage that which can only come from other relationships. I try to explain as clearly as possible that the ideal situation is when one is plugged into many networks of people and gets different rewards from different relationships. I explain to patients that, besides the marital relationship, ideally one should also be connected to family of origin, nuclear family, friends, colleagues, neighbors, community, etc.

The metaphor serves several functions. First, it suggests that the solution is not "more of the same" or "trying harder" in the relationship; rather, the partner needs to branch out and seek additional relationships (circuits) with others. Another implication of this metaphor is that when partners expect from spouses that which can only come from relationships with others, an "overload" will result. Also implied is that one must protect the marital relationship, which often runs fine on 110 volts, and that if there is excessive voltage available, new circuits must be used or formed.

A final implication is the parallel between electrical terminology and the human nervous system. It is not by accident that we use metaphors from electricity when we talk about our feelings. Terms such as "overload," "blow a fuse," "juiced up," "shocked," "wired," "light up," "resistance," suggest that we often think of our nervous system and our feelings in electrical terms, and we may use this metaphor because the language is correct.

Mistakes husbands make

A corollary to the above is something I often observe about husbands. For reasons which remain obscure to me, I find that many husbands depend exclusively upon their wives for a network rather than developing multiple networks of their own. There really is no problem with this in a marriage as long as it is mutually agreed upon and rewarding for both partners.

The problem with such an arrangement occurs when a husband gets into a fight with his wife and temporarily loses his support system. If the wife has separate networks of support, then the husband is at a huge disadvantage since the wife has people to talk to and receive support from, while the husband might have to wait until the fight is over to regain his support. There are clear advantages in having a network of support besides your spouse. This is the recommendation I make to husbands with a metaphorical story about "mistakes husbands make."

7

STAYING AFLOAT IN
DANGEROUS WATERS

This chapter covers some of the issues involved when psychotherapists become anxious in the treatment session about a clinical case. Since not much effective psychotherapy can go on when a therapist is anxious, it is necessary for the therapist to have some ready remedies for anxiety. The first part of this chapter deals with therapist anxiety created by suicide threats, while the remainder of the chapter deals with other sources of therapist anxiety.

PLACING FAMILIES ON SUICIDE WATCH

Recently, while presenting a case at a conference (1983c), I made an incidental comment about placing a patient's family on suicide watch if and when the patient mentions suicide. From the subsequent questions it soon became apparent that some therapists were unfamiliar with using a suicide watch as an intervention to prevent suicides and to mobilize families. The purpose of this section is to explain the rationale for using a suicide watch, outline how it works, and offer some indications and contraindications for its use in clinical situations.

Before describing a suicide watch, however, let me make some statements about my clinical views on suicide threats, gestures, and maneuvers. I see a suicide threat the same way I see any symptom in a system: First, it is an attempt (con-

scious or unconscious) to maintain equilibrium in a system
which is in transition from one developmental stage in a family's life cycle to another. The identified patient is attempting
to emotionally separate and grow up from the family of origin
and at the same time to protect the family from this change.

Second, the suicide threat, like many symptoms, has a
metaphorical message, and that is that the identified patient
and the family are in considerable pain and under almost unbearable stress, mostly due to experienced or anticipated systems changes.

Third, the suicide threat is a very powerful – and I might
add nasty – way for the patient to immobilize not only the
family, but also, and more importantly, the therapist. By
blocking the therapist's interventions with a suicide threat,
the patient protects the family by postponing the change that
was occurring within the patient and/or the family.

It is both dangerous and anti-therapeutic for a therapist
to feel or become responsible for a patient when a suicide
threat is made while the patient is in treatment. Often, an
overresponsible or inexperienced therapist will be pulled into the patient's or family's emotional system and feel that he
is the only person in the world who will be able to "save" the
patient. Although this therapist is not aware of it, he then
becomes a pawn in a much more extensive system dedicated
to maintaining some form of homeostasis in the family. An
example will suffice.

This hypothetical case involves Sally, a 31-year-old unmarried social worker who seeks individual counseling because
she's depressed, lonely, and would like to find a partner and
start a family. Sally has been in treatment for 12 years with
six different therapists. Early in the first session it becomes
clear to this therapist that Sally is a parentified child (which
may be true of many therapists) who is fused with her parents. Since her sister is married and living in the Yucatan,
she is the only child living near the parents. If Sally got married, she would emotionally move a little away from her parents and then the parents would have to deal with their own
marriage, which until now has been balanced by their mutual
worry about Sally and Sally's depression.

Since Sally's problems stabilize her parents' marriage, she has never been able to separate from them. In the past she has made efforts to separate by emotionally cutting off from these parents. This has left her isolated and lonely, which also contributes to her depression. In addition, the fusion with her parents keeps her from developing or maintaining a relationship with a potential partner (since her choice of married men or the way she relates to available men usually leads to her having unsuccessful experiences). Out of this isolation and depression, she seeks a psychotherapist who will help her.

Now, most experienced systems therapists will recognize that, with her impressive history of treatment failure, Sally is not looking for treatment, but rather, for another homeostat to stabilize her family's system. Sally's isolated and depressed position stabilizes Mama and Papa's marriage (since they worry about her). When the therapist attempts to "help" Sally, he is actually stabilizing the family system by forming the third leg of a triangle between Sally and her parents.

A strategic therapist would give Sally homework which would be directed towards helping her emotionally separate from her parents. Sally would cooperate with these assignments up to a certain point and then stop when she thought she was emotionally separating in a way which would alarm her parents. She would bring the progress to a standstill by changing therapists, dropping out of treatment, or remaining in treatment and "showing" suicide statements. Here the word "show" is used to point out that this is a maneuver and a message to the therapist, rather than the "real thing" (Palazzoli et al., 1978).

I do not want to get into the complicated and important issue of knowing when a suicide statement from the patient is a maneuver and when it is not. Experienced therapists know the difference, the way an experienced baker knows that on a particular day the dough feels like it needs more flour than the amount called for in the recipe. Inexperienced therapists should take no chances and insure that real suicide threats are not ignored.

All therapists know what it feels like when a patient says that she is planning to do herself in. When I hear such statements, I have both very strong personal reactions and some clinical thoughts. First I react with a great deal of anxiety, and later with some anger. I don't want the patient to kill herself, and certainly not while she is in therapy *with me*. I also do not like worrying about patients or getting middle-of-the-night phone calls. As a therapist, my job is to teach people to take care of themselves. My job is *not* to take care of people or to keep them from committing suicide.

The clinician in me realizes that the anxiety aroused by the suicide threat has effectively immobilized me, my thinking, and the therapeutic momentum of the therapy directed towards helping this patient separate from her family. Further, this maneuver has quite cleverly and powerfully stopped the system changes which were about to take place.

The question becomes: *What do I, the therapist, now do to get myself out of this immobilized position?*

One option available to a therapist is to talk about hospitalization or to actually hospitalize the patient. This always has a powerful effect on the patient. At one level, the therapist is saying, "Since you are threatening to take your life, and you cannot take care of youself, we must find others to take care of you and keep you from taking your life." If the patient is "really" going to kill herself, then the hospital staff will be responsible for preventing the suicide, since they are available to watch the patient 24 hours a day. Even if the suicide statement is a maneuver, hospitalization is not a bad idea, since it becomes a message to the patient from the clinician, namely, "If you try to immobilize me with suicide talk, then you will force me to hospitalize you," which I suspect most suicide-threatening patients do not want or expect to hear. The agenda of some suicidal patients is to slow down or stop the therapeutic change from taking place in their family system. Getting locked up in a hospital, infantilized in the typical way in which suicides must be treated in hospitals, is probably one of the last things the suicidal patient has in mind.

The other option available to the clinican is the suicide watch. I have successfully used the suicide watch in different ways with different families. Although patients' and families' reactions to the watch vary, in most cases the end result is that I am able to escape the immobilized position and continue the treatment.

The suicide watch ritual

The suicide watch ritual basically consists of telling a family or a spouse that the patient has talked about or has threatened suicide and that this patient must be watched 24 hours a day until the danger has subsided. Family members can be told this in a treatment session or over the phone, depending upon what the therapeutic contact with these others happens to be. When I fear that a suicide might take place, I make sure that I first tell the patient what I am about to do. This is to insure that the patient does not feel betrayed by me, and that contacting the family is being done to protect rather than to betray the patient. If I were seeing an individual patient alone and he threatened suicide, I would, after placing the family or spouse on watch, see the whole family or the couple in treatment. Thus, the individual therapy would become couple or family therapy.

Let us return to Sally. As Sally continued to emotionally separate from her parents, she began talking of suicide. In this instance I had seen the parents during an initial interview, so I had had some contact with them. Upon hearing about the suicide threat, I told Sally that I would have to call her parents on the telephone and place them on a suicide watch.

When Sally heard this, her anxiety skyrocketed. (In retrospect, if she had as much anxiety about her own life as she had about her parents' reaction to being placed on suicide watch, she would not have been so stuck.) The patient then pleaded with me not to call her parents and promised me that she would never talk about suicide again. I agreed not to call at that time.

Why did the threat of placing the family on suicide watch neutralize the threat of suicide? Frankly, I can only guess at this. The most important thing for me was that the threat of a suicide watch freed me. Once I mentioned calling the parents, the patient became more anxious and I became less anxious. This shift in anxiety placed me in charge again – and if change is to take place using a brief therapy model the therapist must be in charge.

Why did the threat of placing the family on suicide watch produce so much anxiety in the patient? There are several possibilities. Perhaps the patient was so protective of the family that she did not want to increase the ongoing family worry. Another possibility is that the infantilizing nature of a 24-hour watch aroused anxiety in a patient who so desperately wanted to grow up emotionally and be an adult. Or maybe the intervention activated the patient's *hubris* or pride, since her family probably already saw her as being less than normal and certainly less than grown up. Therefore, notifying the family that the daughter was about to take her life would provide further justification for the family's excessive concern about the daughter.

As I have said earlier, I can only speculate on the possible reasons why the watch produced anxiety in this patient. From a pragmatic point of view, the most important thing is that the threat of a family suicide watch reduced the anxiety of the *therapist*; once that was reduced, the therapist could again be a therapist and continue to enhance the changes which were taking place in the family before the suicide threat was made.

What does placing a family on suicide watch do for a system, and how does it have therapeutic value? I suspect that the watch does different things in different systems, but I will speculate on these possibilities.

1) The watch brings the patient together with the family, and then *the entire family* becomes part of the treatment. Or, stated somewhat differently, the therapy changes from individual to couple or family therapy.
2) The family rather than the therapist becomes responsible for watching and insuring that the patient will not take his life. This is important, since it prevents the

therapist from taking a homeostatic position. It also may shake up some underlying assumptions and raise questions about who is responsible for whose behavior. In a linear way, one could argue that Sally is in a fix because she emotionally feels responsible for her parents' survival or happiness. She takes charge of her parents' marriage because her parents cannot or will not. If Sally is in charge of her parents' marriage, she can't get married herself. So instead, she marries a therapist. This doesn't work either, and in time, as the system escalates, the naive therapist may feel responsible for Sally if she threatens to kill herself. The suicide watch pulls the parents back into the therapeutic system to help their daughter – and eventually themselves.

3) The anxiety produced by the suicide threat gets distributed more equally among family members, rather than concentrated on one therapist. (As a therapist I have always been interested in sharing with others.)

4) Bringing the family members together and making them watch the patient mobilizes them to begin to become responsible for what is happening in their family (which includes the patient). For example, the watch might "force" parents who normally take "helpless" positions to become more active, forthright and responsible in preventing their child from taking his or her life.

5) There may be a therapeutic ritual involved here which involves a Hobson's choice for the family. The suicide watch requires the family to keep an eye on the patient 24 hours a day until there no longer exists the possibility of a suicide; this task might become so tedious, boring, and confining that the family might then choose to deal with family issues systemically related to the suicide threat.

For example, let's argue that Sally is depressed out of loneliness, out of her need to have her own family and yet protect her parents and their marriage. Sally is tuned in to the covert marital struggle of her parents, while overtly her parents claim that their marriage is fine and there is no need to change. Placing these parents on a 24-hour watch might become so toxic and tedious for the parents that after a while they will begin to deal with their differences as a less painful and boring alternative.

In addition, bringing the family or couple closer together to perform this watch might make the covert conflict overt, since the watch disrupts and changes the normal way in which the family is organized around closeness and distance. If and when the conflict erupts in the treatment session, the issue can be dealt with by the therapist.

When I am working with a patient who talks about suicide in individual treatment, I use another tactic. Confronted by a powerful suicide gesture, I ask the patient to give me the names and telephone numbers of 10 immediate family members (mother, father, sibs) and extended family members (grandparents, aunts, uncles, cousins). I tell the patient that I need to know the names and phone numbers of these people so I can call them in the event the patient becomes suicidal and needs to be placed on a suicide watch.

Now some may ask, "What do you do when there is a suicide threat from a patient in individual treatment who is unconnected to family?" Here I take a totally dogmatic point of view and say that *all* symptoms are contextual. If the suicide threat is not playing a role in the relationship between the patient and the therapist, then it must be understood in some other social context. If a patient in individual treatment is threatening suicide and has no immediate family, there are always extended family. If no extended family exists, there are other contexts — neighbors, fellow employees, community, religious organizations — which can become activated to take some of the responsibility.

I might remind the reader that not only is suicide a violation of many religious laws, but it is also illegal. As a last resort, if there are no family members to mobilize, you can call the police. The police will usually give the threatener the choice of going to a hospital or jail.

I received a phone call from a woman who was studying family therapy at the Ackerman Institute. Her brother was calling her every day because the brother's wife's sister was threatening suicide. Now the brother's wife's sister was married, but the husband was a gambler who did not respond to the wife's threats of suicide. I first asked whether the couple was interested in therapy; this was suggested but they were not interested.

Rather than seek therapy, the suicide threatener keeps calling her sister, who bothers her husband, who calls his sister (because she is a family therapist trainee), who calls me. There is clearly something wrong here. The suicide threatener does not pursue the most responsible course and get herself into treatment. Instead, she tries to stabilize the marriage with a call to her sister, who then brings her husband in, who then calls the sister.

As a stranger to this entire family chain, I know that the last thing I am going to do is to get on this conga line. I am being asked over the phone what to do – I don't know this case, nor in fact am I that interested, since the person talking to me is so far removed from the problem. The anxiety in this system, as it goes down the line, is too far removed from its original source.

One option is to have the suicide threatener call me. However, I am not interested in the case for a number of reasons, so I don't do that. What I end up doing is telling the calling family therapist to tell the brother that when the suicide threatener begins her number the brother should call the cops.

This is exactly what happened, and a few weeks later I received a note from the brother thanking me for my time and advice. I'm still unsure about what happened, but it appears than the anxiety chain was at least momentarily disrupted. In retrospect, it was an appropriate recommendation, since the woman was not interested in therapy; the suicide situation then rightly became a police matter.

The above clinical examples are but a few of the many ways in which a suicide threat or maneuver has the potential of creating anxiety in the therapist. The most important point I wish to make is that when the therapist becomes anxious, the patient is in charge of the treatment. And when this happens, treament becomes postponed. On the other hand, individuals who use suicide threats and maneuvers are "big gamblers" and are willing to take big chances. I don't think clinicans have to take any risks with such patients; therefore, clinicians unsure of the patient, the maneuver, or the situation should do whatever they have to do to insure that the suicide threatener does not hurt him- or herself.

REDUCING THERAPIST ANXIETY

When I am teaching or supervising a therapist who is stuck with a patient or a family, I ask myself and the therapist, "What is making the therapist anxious?" I focus on this question because I know that when the therapist is anxious the therapy is delayed or postponed or will not go as well as when the therapist is not anxious. Ultimately, the therapist and his or her supervisor must always be respectful of the magnitude and sources of therapist anxiety, particularly when that anxiety is going to interfere with effective treatment.

Sometimes the presence of anxiety is helpful and fruitful, because it elicits something new and emotional in the therapist and/or supervisor, giving both of them additional opportunities to learn and change. Other times the source of anxiety appears contextual – for example, when a therapist is seeing a family with a history of violent escalations, or when a family brings handguns to treatment sessions, or when it becomes evident that a family is connected to organized crime. In the Brief Therapy Project we use to tease each other by talking about how powerful some paradoxical interventions could be – but never as powerful as bullets. I suspect that when a therapist is overwhelmed by anxiety, the sources of that anxiety are probably contextual as well as personal. The focus of this section is on some of the ways in which therapist anxiety can be reduced.

Prepaid sessions as a solution

I became anxious about the possibility that a young schizophrenic I was treating would throw an ashtray through the new one-way mirror in my office. This never scared me before, so I looked into why I found this so upsetting. I quickly realized that this was my new office – my nicely furnished, first office – and I didn't want this patient throwing ashtrays through my one-way mirror. In addition, since this was my first office, it was also a "trial run" or litmus paper, a metaphor of whether I was going to make it economically in private practice and be free of institutional work settings. Was I going to make it in the tough New York psychotherapy industry with the professional grownups? What was making me anxious was that this schizophrenic with a heavy ashtray in her hand was ready to throw it though the one-way window and, in my mind, take away my professional autonomy and validation.

As in most cases, the anxiety was contextual *and* personal. The patient was eyeing this heavy glass ashtray I bought from Murano, Italy, and I was eyeing her eyeing the ashtray, and she knew I was eyeing her eyeing of the ashtray. As long as this was happening, she was in charge of the session.

This patient also had the habit of running out of the treatment room whenever something was said that bothered her. Since in most instances she was the topic of discussion, by running out of the room she continued to control the session and the therapy.

I dealt with this situation by making sure that the treatment session was paid for in advance with some of the patient's own money. Then I had the family and the patient place money in an escrow account for damages to my office. After both these things were accomplished, I knew that the patient could end the session whenever she pleased. This would now become her loss rather than mine, since the session was prepaid. I also was less fearful of my one-way mirror being smashed, since the patient had an investment in keeping that mirror whole. As soon as my anxiety about these issues was reduced in this way, I was better able to help this patient in treatment.

Incidentally, many families will give the therapist a signal about how they will try to control the treatment. Usually, whatever makes the experienced therapist very anxious about the family should tip the therapist off to an issue or a maneuver the family will use to control the treatment. Therefore, therapists should see this as something that goes with the territory, as well as a way for the family to stay in charge and maintain the present homeostasis. At one level, change resulting from effective treatment will produce anxiety, and one way to reduce the family's anxiety is for the family to do something which will raise the therapist's anxiety. Families, by the way, do not intentionally give signals in some preplanned or deliberate way. Nevertheless, they do give the therapist nonverbal signals, which all therapists should respect and take into account.

Rent a marine

Sometimes, family members try to control each other and the therapist with the threat of violence. Experienced therapists normally are able to keep potential escalations in treatment sessions from becoming violent. However, it depends on the level of violence, how well and quickly the family can escalate, and the level of therapist experience.

When violence is used to threaten me in a session, one of my first impulses is to encourage it. I might do one of many things, such as: tell the family that this will be a new and rich experience for me; indicate that I recently bought this new insurance policy from this shady insurance agent whom I don't trust, and that with some genuine violence in the session, we can test out the policy to see if I can collect; talk about hearing about this kind of violence in family therapy, but never having witnessed it myself; get the family to make bets or place odds on who is going to punch whom, how hard, etc.; even wrestle with most anyone under 100 pounds. If the violence doesn't scare me that much, I will attempt to dissipate it in some humorous or paradoxical way.

When I am really scared that violence will erupt in the family, there are some options available. One of the first things that comes to mind is to invite members of the third generation to the next session. Bringing in the grandparents often will keep escalations from becoming violent. It's a professional variation of "if you hit me, I'm going to tell your mother!" Most families will not escalate to physical violence in the presence of the grandparents, unless, of course, the grandmother is Ma Barker. Then the therapist is in trouble.

If the family refuses to bring in family members from the third generation, and I suspect violence will erupt in the next session, I will tell the family that they should not come to the next session unless they also bring some hired "muscle," in the form of a security man, Pinkerton man, or even a marine, in order to make sure that no one gets hurt. The most important thing here is:

1) The therapist should not be intimidated by the threat of violence in the session.
2) The therapist should require the family to hire muscle (at the family's expense) if and when violence is threatened.
3) The family must get a clear message from the therapist that the therapist will not be controlled in this manner.

Spouse abuse

Sometimes therapists get intimidated by the violence displayed in a marital relationship. Because of the high degree of emotionality displayed in this dance, some therapists lose therapeutic leverage by taking sides or attempting to reduce the violence and/or protect the abused one. When the thera-

pist takes sides in this dance, it is the therapist who is usually
more endangered than either spouse.

When the issue of partner abuse comes up in treatment,
I immediately ask the abused one what she (or he) has to do
to make the other partner so crazy that he (or she) gets violent. The abused partner usually shares a knowing smile with
me and the other partner when this question is asked. In no
way am I sympathetic toward the couple's game that the
abused one is a true victim of the abusing spouse. This often
is a systems game, a collusion, where it *appears* as if we have
a real, causal, linear problem with a battered victim and one
mean bastard or bitch, an evil person doing terrible things to
a victim. This marital dance masks the fact that the partners
are not yet married to each other because they are still married to or not emotionally separated from their respective
families of origin.

With this kind of couple, I quickly ask who in their families of origin would appear endangered if the abuse stopped
and the spouses really got along? In time, my goal is to put
a halt to the ongoing vicious partner abuse game and put that
game in the service of each of the partner's family of origin.
In other words, often the couple sees the violence only as a
product of their marital difficulties rather than some quiet
loyalty to their respective families of origin. A subsequent
goal would be to help the partners emotionally separate from
their respective families of origin, so they can emotionally
grow up and decided to either get married or get divorced.
Partner abuse may be a very dramatic way of regulating dis-
tance/closeness in a marriage. It is also sometimes a way of
maintaining passion in relationships.

Getting your marital partner to beat you up may be a way
of maintaining some multigenerational loyalty and family
tradition. A young wife who gets beaten up by her husband
may be replicating a emotional context by being beaten the
way she was beaten by her mother, who was similarly abused
by her parent. Some have speculated that the love was confused with beating. My sense is more systemic; that is, the
more you're "abused" by a parent, the more you remain loyal

to that family in your attempts to undo that abuse. So it's quite likely that a woman or man marries someone who has abuser potential, so they can replicate the relationship the abused one had with the parent in order to undo it. In addition, as long as one is abused by a spouse, one remains loyal to the parents since the abuse itself keeps the marital couple from getting closer.

My point is that this is a marital dance, a game, and the clinician should not be seduced by the unbalanced way in which this couple presents itself. Systemic questions to the victim on how she or he accomplished this feat usually will help the clinician out of this trap.*

It is important to underscore the point that all victims are not necessarily eliciting the abuse. For example, it could very well occur that a wife selects a mate who will abuse her for systemic reasons, but eventually changes and no longer needs to be a victim. The *quid pro quo* changes, and the wife no longer is willing to participate in this old marital dance, nor does she care to be abused. In such cases, the marital relationship might end when the wife walks out. If the abuse continues because the wife can't leave, the clinican must then deal with the systemic reasons for this continued abuse.

Paying treatment fees
following each session

One of the ways in which families or patients can control me and make me anxious is by not paying their bill. This form of control does not happen frequently, but when it does I find it very powerful and unnerving. The person not paying the bill is usually furious, mostly towards the therapist, usually over clinical issues such as the wife's leaving the husband or the child's no longer being symptomatic.

---

*Police making calls know too well about this game, when they attempt to arrest the abuser and the victim refuses to press charges. The abuser is then released until another call comes into the police. Lawyers too are greatly frustrated by this game, when they advise abused partners to change the locks on the door after the abuser is thrown out, which the victims are unable to do.

For example, in the case of Fido (see Chapter 2), I eventually got the mother and the stepfather to establish disciplinary boundaries and Fido shaped up behaviorally. Presently he is doing quite well in boarding school (Fido had previously been thrown out of five boarding schools).

Soon after Fido become asymptomatic, father broke up with his girlfriend (looks like Fido was guarding father's backyard). Anyway, father, two years later, still owes me $500.00, his share of the therapy cost, after it was divided equally between him and the stepfather. In ways, father's anger towards me, expressed through withholding payment, is a bit healthier than Fido's acting out father's anger towards mother. Father may also be angry with me because he no longer has the same access to his ex-wife, since Fido is much less of a problem.

As can be seen, when anger is released by therapy in such intense systems, the therapist may get some of it. One of the more painful ways in which a therapist can experience that anger is through the patient's withholding payment.

Recently, Kitty LaPerriere (1984) was talking about how in most cases the therapist colludes in some way with the patient or family, which may lead to the nonpayment of fees. In the Fido case, my collusion involved not paying enough attention to the fact that I was stepfather's therapist and not father's therapist. I was being brought in by stepfather to make Fido asymptomatic. By succeeding, I took Fido and ex-wife away from father. So why shouldn't father be angry with me?

Perhaps one of the ways to avoid colluding with a family such as Fido's is to collect the fee at the end (or sometimes the beginning) of each session. If the family cannot afford this, the clinician should postpone the session until they can afford the treatment. This may sound heartless, but I think a therapist who is covertly angry and resentful about not getting paid and trying to make believe he is not resentful or

that the resentment is not interfering with the treatment is
fooling himself. Many times the therapist is better off (therapeutically, emotionally, and financially) seeing a family less
often and getting paid each time, rather than seeing a family more often and colluding with nonpayment. The less a therapist colludes this way, the less he or she will feel taken by
the client. As many experienced therapists know, therapist
resentment towards patients for nonpayment of fees is as un-
helpful for successful treatment as therapist anxiety.

Using cotherapists and teams

Sometimes a therapist does not know *why* he is anxious
about a family. If the anxiety does not subside after the therapist sees a family *and* continues to get in the therapist's way
in conducting the treatment, then the therapist should seriously consider inviting a cotherapist or a team of colleagues
to observe a session. The cotherapist or team can be brought
in for a consultation or for treatment. The cotherapist or team
can keep the therapist somewhat meta to the anxiety that
is getting in his way. I think it is important:

1) For therapists to be respectful of their anxiety and to
   attempt to understand and eliminate it so the treatment can continue.
2) When this is not possible, for the therapist not to be
   shy or stubborn and to ask for help—in the form of
   either a consultation or a team.
3) For the therapist to use the cotherapist or team until
   the source of anxiety is known or eliminated.
4) For therapists to be able to get something for themselves from the anxiety experience.

Since I videotape many of my sessions, if and when I get
anxious and/or stuck, I can give the cassette of the last session to my colleagues, who usually can get me unstuck in less
than five minutes. Since my colleagues and I share similar
theory and language, just sharing with them the meta ex-

perience of viewing the tape is usually sufficient to generate
a few ideas about how and why I am stuck. Getting stuck,
by the way, will happen independently of the therapist's experience level because families are powerful emotional systems which sometimes entrap therapists – experienced or not.
Also, therapists can become vulnerable to "this or that" about
a particular family and lose leverage. Having a good lifeguard
on call is always comforting when the therapist chooses to
swim with barracuda.

Reducing contexual replications for therapists

I have found when supervising therapists that they sometimes become stuck with a family because there is a contextual replication; that is, the family being treated is stuck in
a way similar to the way the therapist is stuck in his or her
own family. Sometimes it is possible to help out the family
and the supervisee at the same time. An example will suffice:

> In one case, I was supervising a psychiatrist who
> was stuck treating a family where the children were
> walking all over the parents. The more the family sit-
> uation was described to me, the clearer it became that
> a straight structural intervention was needed – some-
> thing to put the parents in charge and help them set
> behavioral limits and consequences for the children.
> Ironically, this therapist was well trained at the Phil-
> adelphia Child Guidance Clinic! So the problem here
> was not the therapist's lack of knowledge, skill, or
> training, but something else.
>
> I gently inquired further and learned from the psy-
> chiatrist that he was the last-born in his family and
> that he usually took a one-down position to his older,
> incompetent brother. He never dared "take charge"
> of a situation, because he felt that would be too hu-
> miliating to his older brother. Consequently, although
> this psychiatrist could achieve, he was to do so quiet-

ly, in an unobtrusive way. This contextual replication appeared presently with the family he was treating, and the therapist was unable to "take charge" of the family by getting the parents to "take charge" of the kids.

In addition, the psychiatrist was buying supervision from me in part because his friend, a psychiatric social worker a few years older than he, was buying supervision (from *my* former supervisor). Things were getting complicated.

To get back to the family, I told the psychiatrist that he had to make the structural move and get the parents in charge of the children. *In addition*, he was to place a picture of his friend, the social worker, on the wall *next to his M.D. diploma*, and whenever he was unsure of himself or scared to take charge in a treatment session, he was to turn to the picture for inspiration and guidance.

In effect, this therapist was involved in a contextual replication with the treatment family, his friend and me. The contextual replication involved the unresolved difficulty he was still having with his older brother. What I did was supervise the therapist on the family, while making his difficulty (his problems being competent and his problems with his brother) absurd by having him post a photograph of his friend (a metaphor for his relationship with his brother) next to his medical degree.

The supervisory intervention seemed to work, because the psychiatrist was able to set structural tasks for the family. In addition, he canceled the next supervisory meeting with me, since he felt he was doing all right with his families!

8

STAYING ALIVE
AS A THERAPIST

Recently I have begun to struggle with the issue of staying alive as a therapist. I realize that this issue has become important to me as a function of where I am in both my professional and my personal life cycles. My experience, while it may not match that of other clinicians precisely, is certainly not unique. Over the years, I have discovered some approaches that enable me to stay alive, to avoid burnout, and to continue to offer families and patients creative solutions to their problems. In this chapter, I will share my ways of getting unstuck and avoiding being devoured by families.

Over the past 18 years, the clinical areas that have interested me most have closely paralleled the various stages and stuck points at which I have been in my personal life. For instance, as I became less somatically oriented and less hypochondriacal in my own life, I became professionally less interested in my dissertation research on the voluntary control of autonomic responses. After I became a college professor (my mother thought that every successful family should have one), I became less interested in being scholarly. In order to maintain my adolescent rebelliousness, I did some research showing that college students were more effective in changing chronic patients than were mental health professionals. After I set up halfway houses in the community for chronic and retarded populations, I was able to leave Massachusetts and return home to New York City where I was raised.

As I fought and struggled to become more differentiated from my family of origin, I became professionally less interested in treating chronic, resistant, and difficult families. As I began to see my world as less combative, hostile, and resistant, I worked with less resistant families, using paradoxical interventions only when I had to and considerably less often than before. Currently, I do therapy with much more use of self, combined with structural-strategic and educational approaches.

As I became less concerned and invested in the cruelty and anger in my own family, I became less invested in the cruelty and anger which keep some resistant families resistant. In Rich Simon's interview with R. D. Laing for the *Networker* (1983), Laing tells the story of asking Bateson one day why the latter stopped working with schizophrenics. Bateson's reply was that he "got out of the whole business with them and what he called their dumb cruelty" (p. 22). For some reason Bateson's reply stayed with me. Here I was, a young turk doing these fancy, systemic, paradoxical interventions with resistant families and showing this work around the country. Bateson's linear, nonsystemic, moralizing statement cut through all my intellectual nonsense and took some of the wind out of my sails with respect to working with these families.

So here I am, writing the last chapter of this book and asking myself, "What now?" Some of my family and personal dynamics have been worked out through the various professional goals I have set and through some of the clinical populations I have treated. Well, I'm not really sure about what will interest me next, but I am now clearer about what I don't like and what I have attempted to do to change what's wrong for me.

At the present time I enjoy treating families, writing, doing training videotapes, and doing training workshops and conferences. Therapy is not a bad way to make a living, and teaching and writing take care of my intellectual and narcissistic needs. What I don't like is when therapy becomes draining, boring, exhausting, or basically a pain in the ass;

this chapter is an attempt to deal with what I have tried to do when that happens.

WORKING WITH MAXIMUM LEVERAGE

One of the things which I find exhausting as a therapist is working harder than the family during the session. Sometimes it seems that I become more motivated to change some families than the families are motivated to change. I now believe that when this situation happens change is unlikely to occur.

I think the phenomenon of a therapist working harder than a family is, in part, a function of where the therapist is in his or her own professional life cycle. When I was a less experienced therapist and still learning the trade, I would see fewer members of a family than I should. My willingness to work with less than "a full deck of cards" came from my needs to see families, to get experience, to be a hero, and to cure families that other therapists couldn't cure. After being "done in" several times and developing more confidence with the experience, I now see families with what I call "maximum leverage for change." Since I am now doing therapy for a living rather than to understand something about myself or my family, I not only have to take better care of myself, but must also be sure that the family works as hard as I do. This will maximize change for the family, as well as keep me alive for a longer period of time.

What do I mean by having maximum leverage for change? Part of maximum leverage is having all the relevant family members in the session, that is, all individuals who seem related to the presenting problem. This gives the therapist maximum information about the system in question. As Carl Whitaker (1976a) has said, "More is always better." There is always more information, as well as more possibility for change, available to a therapist when there are more family members in a session than when there are fewer.

This approach requires giving considerable thought to the issue of who is invited to the first session. For example, if I learn during the initial phone call that the symptom is psychosis, I tell the family that I need to see the psychotic, the sibs, the parents and the grandparents on both sides. I think both Murray Bowen (1978) and Carl Whitaker (1976a) are absolutely correct when they say that it takes three or more generations to produce a psychotic. Further, it is my sense that it takes the presence of three generations in the first session to undo a psychotic, if you wish to undo a psychotic in the first treatment session.

Younger or less experienced family therapists may have the same reaction I did when I first read Bowen and Whitaker. They might say something like, "How arrogant of them — and besides, I'll never get the family to bring in three generations, so I must work with what they do bring in," or "Well, Murray and Carl are big shots, and they can pull this off, but I'm a little dandelion." Naturally, if a therapist sees himself or herself as a dandelion, he or she will come off that way to a family, and the family, rather than the therapist, will then dictate who comes to the session. I am repeatedly surprised by how often three generations will appear for that first session. When there is difficulty, I suspect it comes as often from the therapist's self-perception as from the resistance in the family.

There is an added bonus to working with three generations in the initial interview: I always have fun with three generations in the room. The identified patient usually stops acting psychotic, a lot of the rage can begin to be appropriately directed and worked out, and the grandparents are as much fun as the patient. The parents are usually the ones who appear resistant to change, but once they are freed somewhat from the grandparents, the patient in third generation can usually prepare to leave home. All the action, suspense, mystery, and information are in one room: This not only makes the work easier, but for me leads to an experience that is often fun, touching, rewarding, and anything but draining or boring. In fact, as many therapists know, a good initial interview with three generations can even be exhilarating. And it's certainly one way to stay alive as a therapist.

An overresponsible, less experienced therapist might feel
that it is unethical to refuse to see a family just because they
won't bring in three generations. My responses to this are
many: 1) Whoever heard of a cardiac patient telling the sur-
geon the specifications required by the patient before the
surgery takes place? 2) This is still a free country, and if a
family is "unable" to bring in three generations, there are
other options available. 3) There will always be therapists out
there who are willing to work with what the family decides
to offer. 4) A family in search of "homeostatic therapy" will
eventually find it.

Another case in which maximizing leverage is the key to
maintaining my effectiveness and therefore my aliveness occurs when someone refers to me a single, unattached, depressed, 36-year-old patient who wants to marry and start
a family. More often than not, the patient has an impressive
history of treatment failure with other therapists. Years ago,
I would see this type of patient individually, often for years.
Although I will not dispute the importance and helpfulness
of individual therapy, in order for me to stay alive these days
I no longer see this kind of patient in individual treatment.
From experience I know that these patients are often alone,
unattached, and depressed because they are still protecting
one or both parents. At some level, these patients uncon-
sciously fear that something dangerous will happen to their
parents if they emotionally separate. So they go through life
consciously and desperately trying to connect while at the
another level sabotaging these efforts.

I can point out to such patients in individual therapy how
and why they cannot connect. I can even coach them Bowen-
style (1978) to emotionally separate from their parents. This
will work; it will take a few years. On the other hand, I can
work faster by first seeing the patient in an initial interview
with the parents and other sibs. I then get a more complete
picture of this family system; also, with more people in the
room I always have more therapeutic possibilities for interventions.

In summary, when working with the individual patient and

his or her family, I can work faster, have more leverage, and see changes more readily – all of which are important for me to stay alive as a therapist. In addition, of course, the individual patient and the family being treated have more opportunity for change.

In a similar vein, if I'm having a difficult time with a couple I will ask them to bring in their parents (Framo, 1981) or their children (Bloch, 1976). The couple is always more interesting and alive in the presence of Grandma and Grandpa and/or the kids. Once I get unstuck with the couple I can choose to continue working with just the couple or to keep other members of the family in the treatment session.

USING TIME INTERVALS AS A SOURCE OF LEVERAGE

From my involvement in the Brief Therapy Project at the Ackerman Institute from 1975 to 1981, I have learned to comfortably use the time interval between treatment sessions as a source of therapeutic leverage. During the years of that project, we were not being paid by the Institute or by the families, and our only investment was in changing resistant families as efficiently and quickly as possible. We were able to experiment with different intervals between sessions, since there was no personal investment in seeing families for income. We often gave homework assignments and therapeutic rituals to these families, and after a while we found that certain time intervals between sessions were needed for the family to digest, understand, and perform the homework and rituals. For example, with chronic, very resistant families, we would not schedule sessions more often than once a month. Usually an assessment of the resistance and the anxiety in the family during a session would in part determine the time interval before the next scheduled session. This is discussed quite clearly in Mara Selvini Palazzoli's paper on time (1980).

In my private practice, I work in a brief, systemic mode. Through experimentation, I have found that couple therapy is best spaced in two-week intervals. Most of time the session runs an hour and half, but sometimes it runs an hour; this depends on how much information I need, as well as on how much I can endure as a therapist. Partners need two weeks to act upon the prescribed homework or rituals, to act differently toward each other and toward their parents (if and when I coach couples to take different positions with their parents). Sometimes they resist doing the ritual the first week, but carry out the homework during the second week. If I see the couple every other week and give homework, there is always new information in each session from the feedback of the homework. There is considerable movement in these two weeks, so I can stay interested in the changes and progress.

Another way to use time as clinical leverage to change families is to make the next session for a particular individual, couple, or family contingent upon a prescribed change taking place. I call this *reverse treatment* because it appears to be the reverse of how traditional treatment works. In typical treatment, a patient theoretically seeks treatment to change. In reverse treatment, a patient must change to earn another session.

For reverse treatment to work, a patient or family must be more motivated to see the therapist than they are anxious about change. I set up reverse treatment with resistant patients who are often covertly looking for a homeostat rather than a therapist. Once a relationship has been developed between the patient and the therapist (and this seduction can take place in the initial session), one can use this relationship as leverage to produce further change. Change is placed totally in the hands of the consumer; the therapist avoids the role of homeostat and remains a therapist. With very resistant families, particularly ones with psychotic members, after the system has shifted and no longer requires someone to be psychotic, I outline the next step which needs to be taken by the family. The subsequent session is then scheduled by the family when this next step is taken. If the next step is not taken, I view this as evidence that the family is not ready and

I won't see them; I thereby reduce the possibility of becoming a homeostat to this system.

An example of reverse treatment follows:

> The patient was a 25-year-old female named Karen who had been psychotic for about three years. The onset of the psychosis occurred just after father left mother and the family and moved to Canada. Attending treatment sessions were Karen, her sister Lydia, age 27, and mother, age 52. The prescription that follows was given to the family at the end of the fourth session of treatment. By this session the chronic patient had not been symptomatic for a few months, and the interaction between the mother and this daughter had shifted significantly. There was very little anxiety (and therefore leverage) in the family or session. In addition, this was the kind of family that could stay in treatment forever. This was my message to them:

> *Mother and Lydia have bossiness and pride which at times are stronger than themselves and which ultimately keep the two women from connecting to others in a meaningful way. Karen knows how bossiness and pride keep the two women isolated, and in a loving and sensitive way becomes psychotic to temporarily expand the family with caring and supportive people in the form of psychotherapists. Thus, the only time mother and Lydia will allow other people to enter this family and support them is when someone becomes mentally ill. The dilemma with this situation is that one has to remain sick in order to enlarge the family with supportive people. The team therefore recommends that, beginning today, mother become more depressed, Karen become psychotic, and Lydia become more isolated from her feelings, her family, and her friends, which will result in bringing more psychotherapists into this family to make everyone feel better but not change anything.*

Now that's the team report. Laraine (Shaw, my cotherapist) and I disagree with the group and we will be willing to negotiate a new contract with the family for additional sessions of family therapy, but only when the family shows a natural increase in size. That implies a new partner in your (anyone of the three women) lives, rather than any one of you becoming pregnant.

Seven months later, I received a call from the family asking for a session, since the family had experienced a natural increase in size. Lydia was now living with a boyfriend.

During this session, it was clear that Mama was anxious and angry about Lydia's having a boyfriend and emotionally moving away from the family. Karen had not been psychotic for some time but was asking about increasing her participation in day treatment from two to five days. The following intervention was then given to the family:

The team is alarmed over the changes which have been made in this family, which have produced too much anxiety, and recommend that things be slowed down a little bit. They feel the best way to slow things down is for 1) Lydia to begin preparing to break up with her new boyfriend and resume the lifeguard position in this family; and 2) Karen to begin to show symptoms, increase day treatment from two to five times a week, and watch Jane (mother's sister) more closely, in preparation for becoming the spinster child in the family. This way Karen and Lydia will be assured in their minds that Mom will be OK.

Laraine and I disagree with the group. The team, however, will not permit us to schedule the next family therapy session until a family member takes her next step towards independence on her own behest, and tells us.

In both interventions, one can see how the family must change before the next session is scheduled, and how they dictate when that takes place. There are various ways in which this can be done, but the basic gist is that the family must progress with a change in their lives in order to "earn" the next session. This strategy probably works best with chronic situations, because it keeps the therapist in a therapeutic position and prevents his falling into the position of being a stabilizing homeostat for a family.

I also use time as clinical leverage when a chronic or resistant family gives me a hard time about making an initial appointment. What usually happens is that I suggest one time, which the family can't make. Another time is given for a week later and that cannot be made. The excuses for not being able to make these sessions are usually vague, obscure, or just plain ridiculous. I then propose a third time and tell the family that, if that appointment cannot be made, my next opening is four to five months later. I specify this by saying, in December, for example, that I have an opening on Monday, May 7th, at 7 p.m. This often gets the family into treatment in December.

Another use of time is based upon a determination during the initial interview of the level of anxiety and resistance in the family system. This is usually a "right hemisphere" determination. If the resistance is greater than the anxiety, I will schedule the next session (if needed) after a longer than the usual interval. For example, if I am normally seeing a chronic, resistant family with an between-session interval of one month, and the resistance is greater than the anxiety during a session, I am inclined to schedule the next session in two or three months. Families must be anxious and always moving towards the therapist (and therapy) to change; if this is not happening, I will increase the between-session interval to whatever period I think is needed to keep the family moving in this direction. If the anxiety level is greater than the resistance, I will maintain the usual one-month interval between sessions.

MAXIMUM LEVERAGE BY
NOT NEEDING PATIENTS

When therapists *need* patients to make a living, some therapists will lose leverage and do therapy differently from when they do *not* need patients to make a living. I am reminded of this when I observe how my interventions, rituals, and homework assignments vary in part depending upon whether my calendar is filled, overfilled, or open. When I have more than enough patients, my interventions are tougher and more powerful; also, I am more willing to pressure my patients to change by not seeing them until a prescribed homework assignment is accomplished or a particular therapeutic goal has been reached. In such instances, I can afford to do this because I do not feel the pressure of making a living (in this way) and having to see a certain number of patients that week.

I think therapists have to make some determination of the personal price they pay when they sit with some patient or family for an hour with nothing going on. For me this experience is painfully boring, and I personally would rather be doing something else. My personal and professional posture in this situation is to discontinue treatment until there is material and motivation for therapy. The time freed by discontinuing treatment with patients who have no material or motivation can be directed toward other ways of making money, such as writing books or articles, giving lectures or workshops, making videotapes, or taking on another part-time, more interesting job. Nonproductive, boring sessions lead me to think that I don't like doing therapy, which in fact is not the case. However, I don't like to be trapped in boring, energy-draining situations, even if I am being paid.

Ironically, the therapist who doesn't need patients or money has much greater leverage for producing change than the therapist who needs patients. Further, therapists who feel trapped into doing therapy sessions when there is no material will be depleted by boredom and will burn out soon. It takes considerable courage to "give up money" and discharge patients, but the price one pays for keeping patients longer than needed is damage to the therapist, as well as to the patients.

I am reminded of case I treated a few years ago. A woman was having some trouble as a single parent to her 10-year-old son. After a few sessions she was no longer having problems with her son and wanted to work on some problems she was having with her parents and brother. After she successfully changed some of her positions with her family of origin, there was little anxiety or material to work on. We could have worked on coupling, but she claimed she was not interested or ready for this.

Her main problem at that point was saying good-bye to me, which was very hard for her because she had become so attached to me. I then told her that I understood her feelings and that she could come as long as she liked, just to chat and schmooze with me. She would, of course, continue to pay the regular fee. The patient liked the idea. The following week, she was ready to terminate treatment.

For the next few years, this patient called now and then just to make sure that I had an open hour for her, in case she needed it, although she didn't need treatment at the time, since things were going well. I told the patient that even if I were booked solid, I would always make room for her. A few years later she came in for a session just to make sure that I agreed with her that she was in love with a guy who would be good for her. We both concurred. It was important for this woman to know that she could confer with me when needed and that the relationship was intact even though she wasn't seeing me regularly. This is a very economical way of working for both the patient and the therapist. It works for the patient because the therapist is there only when needed. It works for the therapist since he is there only when there is material and anxiety.

VARYING THE LENGTH OF SESSIONS

There is nothing sacred about the 50-minute hour, although it is useful for organizational and economic purposes. One of the things I do to both maximize therapeutic leverage and stay alive as a therapist is to vary how time is used, rather than letting an arbitrary time-frame dictate treatment.

For example, when I schedule a consultation or the first treatment session, I leave close to two and a half hours open for the interview. If I do not have a working hypothesis and an intervention for the family at the end of the initial interview, I will schedule an additional two-hour consultation. This allows me to get as complete a picture as possible before I intervene with an interpretation, a homework assignment, or a ritual. Once I have my hypothesis, I can assign some meaningful ritual, which will start the therapy off in an interesting and powerful way.

One of my recurring fantasies about staying alive as a therapist involves practicing psychotherapy the way a physician conducts a medical practice. This would mean scheduling and seeing a patient for as long as needed, prescribing the next step, and finishing the "examination" when it was completed, rather than at the end of a scheduled hour.

> One day when I was thinking about this issue, I asked a patient how she would feel about coming in for a session and staying for whatever time period was needed for me to find out how she was doing and how she did the prescribed homework. Following this, she would receive the next assignment and the session would end. If the session ended before the 50-minute hour was over, that would be fine, and the fee would be adjusted accordingly. If the session took more time than 50 minutes, similar adjustments would be made.
>
> After thinking about this, my patient told me that, although she liked the efficiency of it all, she preferred to get her 50 minutes' worth, even if the new homework for the next session was assigned 15 minutes

into the session. When asked why she preferred this, she said that she "liked talking to me and wanted the 50 minutes she paid for."

In this instance it is quite clear that the relationship was very important to the patient. Then the question becomes: Does the patient change because the strategic homework was "correct" and "effective" or did the patient do the homework because of the relationship she had with me? Perhaps she did the homework because she liked me and wanted my approval. As a strategic therapist, I sometimes forget about the importance of the relationship between the therapist and the patient, although the research has always supported the notion that the "therapist" variables appear to be more or equally as important as the theory of change.

Sometimes simply controlling the use of time can enable the therapist to maintain his equilibrium:

> A patient I was seeing in individual therapy proclaimed one day that this was her hour and that she could do with it whatever she liked. I quickly and gently reminded her, first of all, that it was 50 minutes rather than an hour. I then went on to tell her that it was *our* "hour" and we could talk about things which we *both* agreed upon. In addition, I reminded my patient that, although it might be her 50 minutes, it was my nervous system being subjected to her for 50 minutes, and that this was clearly not a free-for-all, where she could do and say whatever she wanted.

USING ONESELF TO STAY ALIVE
AND CREATE CLINICAL LEVERAGE

In 1969, while teaching a course in family therapy, I encountered the "Hillcrest" family.* The Hillcrest series, showing four separate clinical interviews with the same family con-

*Available from Psychological Cinema Register, Pennsylvania State University, University Park, PA 16802.

ducted by Nathan Ackerman, Murray Bowen, Carl Whitaker, and Don Jackson, is a good way to introduce students to the field of family therapy.

During one of the interviews, Carl Whitaker tells the family that he wants to get something out of the interview for himself. When I first heard Carl say this, my reaction was, "What a selfish son-of-a-bitch. Here's this poor, struggling family in enormous pain, and the therapist wants something from the session for himself." Fifteen years later, I completely understand what Carl was saying. My thinking 15 years ago was naive, reflecting an all-or-none mentality that said you couldn't help a family and yourself at the same time. My thinking has changed since then. From my clinical experience and my contact with Carl Whitaker (see his article on staying alive, 1976b), I have realized that I must continue to grow as a person and as a therapist and that this growth involves an interactional process that is ultimately beneficial to both my patients and myself.

Having fun and using humor

As far as I know, there is no commandment that says a therapist must endure suffering and sometimes abuse in a treatment session directed towards helping others. When I am in a treatment session, I am, of course, focused on helping a family change, but I am also out to have some fun. Not only do I need to have fun and be playful, but sometimes, if I can get away with it, I also try to push the fun and play to joy. I'm doing this for me, but I suspect there are also clinical spin-offs that work therapeutically towards change.

Humor is a vital part of my therapeutic approach. With some patients, I may trade the latest jokes going around town, usually at the beginning or end of the session. Or we might discuss the latest outrageous event in New York, or just plain gossip about this or that. Sometimes we will do this for five minutes, other times for 20 minutes. Other times the entire session is spent in such "small talk"; later on in treatment, the patient may indicate that this particular "wasted" session was very important to him.

Usually the patient will get to work when he or she is ready. With less chatty or more serious patients, I get to work immediately, and I do this primarily for me, not the patient. (Did you ever try to stay chatty with a serious patient? Very serious work.) In general, usually by mutual agreement, part of the session is completely social, and this helps me stay alive as a therapist.

From my position in my family of origin, one of my needs in a social and/or tense context is to be funny. I am sure that humor was used in my family of origin to cut the tension, depression, and boredom. Or, to express it more systemically, one of my roles in my family was to counterbalance too much pain or boredom. Since I was validated by my family for this, this tendency has persisted and I continue to use humor to counterbalance excessive pain in my life and in my work.

One of the life-saving qualities of humor is that it powerfully changes the ongoing affect in a social context. It also brings a different light to what may seem painfully depressing, despairing, or hopeless. By changing the contextual affect in a treatment session, the therapist also regains control of the session, which may have been slipping away because of prevailing despair.

> In an individual therapy session, I was feeling more and more controlled by the patient's verbalized "depression" and "ambivalence." Finally, no longer able to restrain myself, I told the patient that if he needed to continue talking about his depression and ambivalence, I would refer him to an ambivalence or depression doctor. If he wanted to continue working with me, he would presently have to tell me where he was stuck. With that he focused on the problem.

One of the things I repeatedly tell my students is that as therapists they must avoid being controlled by the family's affect in the session. If the family is too serious, the therapist should shift to lightness or humor, and if the family is too funny about something serious, the therapist should become serious, etc.

Humor provides the intellectual stimulation *I need* in the session. There are always hundreds of ways that a depressing reality can be reframed; the challenge of finding funny and sometimes outrageous reframings keeps me intellectually alive.

When I was in individual treatment, my therapist, Ian Alger, laughed *with me* and *at me* for about two years. The combination of his sense of humor and the respect I had for him helped me abandon an overserious therapeutic stance. There was something comforting about a benign authority figure laughing (and sometimes giggling) over my seriousness and complaints. After a while, I was too embarrassed to bring up my diddly complaints, and in time I myself became bored with them. I am convinced that Ian's laughter with and at me was his way of staying alive, as well as a powerful message to me to lighten up and become less serious.

Finally, being funny is entertaining and reflects, in part, my need to entertain, be liked, and laugh with others. Some of my patients call me or come in for a treatment session with no problems in their lives. They either miss me or want to have a good laugh and come in just for that. Of they might call me for five minutes, just to touch base or share a joke.

Metaphor

Another way in which I try to stay alive as a therapist comes from my need to use metaphors. Metaphors are very rich, dramatic, and three-dimensional. They not only contain a visual picture, but they also have a message and emotions tied to them; when they are used by a experienced clinician who is talented with metaphors, the therapeutic impact is powerful.

A few examples will suffice:

> When I was in treatment, I saw the world in a quite dichotomous way: black and white, good and bad, right and wrong. One day my therapist likened this thinking to the lining up of concentration camp

victims who, when directed towards the left, would go to a work camp, and when directed to the right would go to the gas chamber. This is an old therapy technique of "contaminating" a fantasy or, in this case, a way of thinking. The therapist used a very powerful, ghastly metaphor to mitigate, neutralize, or contaminate a very powerful, rigid way of thinking. After that contamination, I learned to see the shades of grey, and I still have very strong negative reactions to black and white thinking.

* * * *

I was treating a couple were both partners had been previously married. In this new family, the wife was setting up a fortress of her own sons (from the first marriage) around her for "distance and safety." The husband was complaining about wanting to get closer to the wife and also wanting some authority over her kids in this new family. The wife was clinging to her children (18- and 16-year-old boys). I gave mother various structural moves to place her in charge of discipline of these two sons, which she was unable to do. (Mother, of course, was using these sons to deal with husband in various indirect ways.)

Finally, after several structural interventions proved unsuccessful, I (impulsively, but quite strategically) asked mother whether she ever thought about having sex with her 18-year-old son? Mother jumped out of her chair when she heard my suggestion. At the following session, mother indicated that she was able for the first time to set boundaries and limits for her sons with some success. I suspect my contaminating metaphor of mother sleeping with son helped her begin to separate from her son and deal with her marital business more directly.

I was raised on metaphors. My maternal grandmother spoke only in metaphor. (She would never say, "Mrs. Smith, our neighbor on the fifth floor." Rather, she would refer to Mrs. Smith in Yiddish as "The Frog" or "The Bell" because Mrs. Smith looked like a frog or had a voice that sounded like a bell.) As a youngster growing up in my family, I remember my father always having difficulty asking for things except in metaphor, and sometimes my mother didn't necessarily mean what she said. In other families, where family members are able to articulate more directly and clearly what they want and mean, there might be less opportunity to practice thinking metaphorically.

For me, metaphor is the music in life, where words are the lyrics. It's three-dimensional, connected to emotions, and always connotes powerful messages. When families I am treating use metaphor, I get very excited and usually try to respond metaphorically to them. Since I see metaphorical thinking as a right-hemisphere phenomenon, when families and I use metaphor, we have "right-hemisphere" conversations, which I find emotionally-connecting, informative, emotionally rich, and fun.

A couple came in for treatment with the presenting symptom being the boyfriend's obsession about putting a knife through his girlfriend. He was frightened about thinking of knives and didn't know what to do.

During the initial session it became clear that the boyfriend had high blood pressure, came from a family where anger was never expressed overtly, and could not express normal anger towards his girlfriend. The following metaphorical intervention was used in a ritual which was given to this couple:

Betty, I think Bob knows how vulnerable you feel about normal couple fighting. And I think because he loves you so much he keeps normal male anger out of your relationship because he knows how sensitive and vulnerable you feel about being a part of a normal couple fight, knowing also how terrified you were about fighting in your own family. And I think he protects you from your vulnerability to normal couple fighting by keeping the anger inside and carrying the anger for both people in the relationship.

And I think he will continue to protect you and restrain himself from showing this anger until he gets signals from you that you care about the relationship enough to start learning to tolerate normal couple anger.

Now, Bob, Betty wants to be the orchestra leader in your relationship together (and she's a pretty good one — she might even make the Philharmonic!). But when she starts orchestrating too heavily, I just want you to tell her, unangrily, that you are blowing your own horn. That means that, as an orchestra leader who wants you included in the orchestra, she will have to start tolerating soloists who do not read the music. And that may be very hard for her.

The following dialogue ensued:

Betty: Of course it will be very hard. That's why sometimes I think it's just easier to stay by myself.

Dr. B.: Well, that may be your decision. But you're never going to become a great orchestra leader because you're never going to get top musicians.

Betty: Well that's not true — I have a son (six years old). I can orchestrate him for another few years . . .

Dr. B.: That's not the same as a professional musician. You may want to be in charge of little musicians playing toy instruments rather than the real thing.

The orchestra metaphor was useful both to the couple and to me as the therapist. By referring to their problem metaphorically, the couple could gather some safe distance from their conflict and still address it at the same time. Staying within the metaphor also added some lightness and play to what appeared to be a rather frightening presenting problem.*

MAINTAINING META POSITIONS
AND META POSTURES

The importance of maintaining some distance from the emotionality of a particular couple or family in treatment has been stressed by many psychotherapists. It keeps the therapist from getting sucked into the emotional process of the family; he or she then has more perspective and consequently more clinical leverage. In addition, I find taking certain meta positions helpful in keeping me alive both as a therapist and as a person.

One meta position I invariably take when doing therapy is to *not take things too seriously*. This is not to say that I am flip about many of the real and painful situations and feelings that are discussed in therapy. I am referring to issues that patients often bring which one can't do much about, or topics which, if discussed, can only lead to additional self-pity; these issues can be dealt with differently depending upon what posture or meta position the therapist assumes.

What keeps popping into my head is an old medical adage my college roommate once shared with me about the clinical problems he sees as a pediatrician. The adage states what I gather is the medical reality: that about 80% of the presenting problems seen in a clinical practice take care of themselves without medical interventions. That is, the immunological, self-healing functions of the human body eventually take care of and correct 80% of all presenting problems. Of the remaining 20%, there is nothing that can be done about 10%, thus leaving 10% that the doctor's treatment can influence.

*An edited videotape is available from the author.

While I do not want to suggest that the same may be true of psychotherapy, I cannot logically or empirically rule it out. I think the good, experienced therapist knows where that possible 10% resides and effectively makes use of his or her skills when the opportunity presents itself. Thinking seriously that one should cure all of life's problems nurtures self-destructive rescue fantasies.

By maintaining a meta position of not taking things too seriously, I am pursuing one of my favorite philosophical postures toward life and therapy, captured in the old Yiddish proverb, "*Mann tracht und Gott lacht*," or "Man plans and God laughs," or, said another way, "Man proposes and God disposes," or, as in an old proverb from the island of Martinique, which translates simply, "Nothing matters." The point is that many problems presented in therapy have to do with some loss of perspective on life; a healthy benevolent, philosophical posture can be quite effective in helping demoralized patients, as well as enabling the therapist to maintain a meta position.

As a therapist I at times assume meta postures, one of which involves *avoiding precious earnestness*. By earnestness, I am referring to the deadly, painful seriousness which can sometimes be observed among some individuals in the helping professions. Some of these workers are depressed people who become alive when entering areas such as dread, emptiness, loss, and rage—and like magnets resonate to such areas. They are also people who unfortunately take themselves very seriously and, as a consequence, have a heavier disposition in life than I prefer to have for myself.

Another meta posture I take is to discourage, whenever I can, deadly, manipulative depression, ambivalence, and whining.

I am reminded of a ritual I gave to a professional whiner and moaner who was getting on my nerves with his self-pity and incessant *kvetching*. Finally, out of exasperation as well as a need on my part to regain control of the therapy, I gave him the following ritual to do each day:

I told the patient that his pain and suffering probably had some deeper ethnic and tribal roots, to which we were not giving enough time and tribute in the therapy sessions, and that his *kvetching* had a rhythmic cant to it that reminded me of the praying of old-fashioned Orthodox Jewish men from Eastern Europe.

So for the next two weeks, each night for 30 minutes, he was to put on his *yarmulke* and *talis* (skull cap and prayer shawl), go to the corner of a room, face East, begin moving back and forth in prayer, and sing his suffering and self-pity out loud in order to get further in touch with his primal roots and background.

Two weeks later the patient reported doing the ritual; however, after a few days he began to laugh uncontrollably and couldn't continue. Not only did the ritual help him stop the self-pity outside the treatment sessions, but more importantly, it also stopped the self-pity and *kvetching* during the session.

Meta postures also reflect what I like to go for when I am doing treatment. When I am conducting a treatment session I look for adventure, intrigue, mystery, mischievousness, surprise, outrageousness, humor, confrontation, and provocation.

When I am about to conduct an initial interview, I feel excited, like a little boy on the night before a big trip. Sometimes I can't fall asleep because of the excitement. So, after 15 years of doing family therapy, what is so exciting about an initial interview? I guess it still is different things to different clinicians. For me, there is always considerable adventure, intrigue, and mystery in an initial interview. The adventure consists of the many possible dangers and riches involved in jumping into the lives of a patient, couple, or family. The intrigue and mystery come from the initial contract between the therapist and the family; that is, there is a problem, and the therapist has been called upon to help the family solve the problem. In addition, the solution is not apparent, and a great deal of sleuthing must be done to help the family "solve the mystery." So, for me there is considerable emotional and intellectual richness, since the initial interview involves placing myself in a multifaceted, sometimes dangerous context and solving the difficult puzzle or mystery that it contains.

If psychotherapy consisted only of initial interviews, I don't think I would have any trouble staying alive as a therapist. Freshness, newness, and uniqueness are always a part of initial interviews. The problem occurs later on, in the middle of treatment, and that is when I must do other things in the session to avoid burnout. I then use mischievousness, outrageousness, playfulness, humor, surprise, confrontation, and provocativeness as a way of keeping a certain energy or hum going in the session.

> One of my favorite rituals is given to a couple where one spouse is complaining about how the other spouse humiliates him or her in public and in front of friends, and how helpless the victim of humiliation has been in stopping the humiliation. Talking or fighting about it does not seem to change things.
>
> After hearing about this humiliation, I tell the couple that I know of only one way for this situation to change. I say that it always works, but that the humiliated spouse must do it, no matter what. In other words, I set up a little devil's pact with the humiliated one before I suggest a solution.
>
> When willingness to do anything is given, I then instruct the humiliated one that, from this moment on, whenever he or she feels humiliated in public by the other spouse, she or he must grab the humiliator by the genitals. The grabbing can be approached from either the ventral or dorsal side (depending upon which side is more available, and also leaving it up to the whim of the grabber).

After the partners recover from a burst of nervous laughter, they agree. They usually return to the next session with this problem solved. In most cases, the humiliator doesn't dare to humiliate the now genital-grabbing spouse in public. And the victim no longer fears being humiliated because a solution is available which can be acted upon if and when humiliation takes place. Since the fear of potential humiliation no longer is an issue, the spouses are in a more balanced position. And as I explain to couples, if genital-grabbing occurs in front of friends, it's more likely to produce envy than any other feeling.

Another case example illustrates the use of outrageousness, as well as metaphor.

I received a referral from a colleague who had become stuck treating a couple. The spouses had been symmetrically struggling for control over many issues and their present struggle was whether their basic problem was psychological or sexual. The wife insisted that it was psychological and the husband that it was sexual. Prior sex therapy was unsuccessful in treating the husband's sexual impotence, and psychological therapy with my colleague was equally unsuccessful.

During the consultation, it became clear that both spouses were still quite enmeshed with their families of origin. The husband still looked to his parents for approval and advice. The wife's mother and father were dead, but she was very involved with her mother's sisters. These four aunts were fat, asexual, men-hating women, from whom the wife still needed approval. I told the wife I suspected that if she had a normal sexual life, these four aunts would be very upset since she admitted that these women probably had not had sex with their wimpy husbands for decades.

I then told the couple how sensitive the husband

was to his wife's need for approval from these aunts, and the possible jealousy that the aunts would feel if they found out that the wife had normal sexual needs and was being gratified by her husband (the implication was that part of the husband's problem with his penis was his sensitivity to his wife's reaction to her aunts in the event the wife was satisfied sexually). Therefore, for the next two weeks, the couple was instructed to do the following ritual: When either the husband or the wife wanted to make love, they were both to stand up next to one another. Both were to monitor the husband's erection. Then the wife was to gently turn the husband around 360 degrees. If the husband's erection was maintained while he was pointed towards his parents' home or towards her aunts' homes (since all four aunts lived in Brooklyn, the direction was northeast from where the couple lived), then it was "safe" to make love. If the erection was lost when pointed towards his parents or her aunts, the couple was to wait for another time, until it was safe.

Despite the seeming outrageousness of this assignment, the couple did the homework for two weeks, with the husband realizing that his penis had more wisdom than his mind. The ritual seemed to rebalance the marital struggle and enabled the couple to focus on other issues.

After the excitement of the initial interview, the therapist can become bogged down in the muddy middle sessions. A playful attitude can be the lifeline to tow the therapist and patient to dry land and get the therapeutic cart moving again.

CONFRONTATION AND PROVOCATION

Confrontation and provocation can be used to get something going or cooking when nothing is happening in the session. When I am bored, I am more likely to stir the pot with a provocative comment than when I am stimulated.

For me it's no problem at all to confront and provoke, because I was raised that way. In fact, I was surprised to learn later in life that everyone else was not raised by provocation. However, I don't think all therapists can get away with adopting a confrontive style just to get something going in a session. Whitaker, Minuchin, Satir, Ackerman and Andolfi are therapists whose personal style includes actively confronting and provoking their patients and families. Such therapists get away with being provocative and do not offend their families because they are able verbally and nonverbally to convey other aspects of themselves as therapists and people. These therapist qualities include warmth, charm, caring, forthrightness, wanting to help, and charisma. Within the context of a caring relationship, a confrontation provides a healthy jolt to enliven a deadly therapy hour.

Often I use persistence in a rather aggressive, provocative way, to get information from patients until I am satisfied that I know everything I need to know. One of my frequent responses to patients' answers of, "I don't know," is, "Yes you do." With considerable persistence on my part, patients and families will eventually verify the working clinical hypothesis I have about how a symptom serves a family system. If my students have learned anything from me in supervision, it is that they give up a line of questioning too quickly, and thus let the family, rather than the clinician, dictate what information is available about the case. As students see how this persistent questioning leads to *additional* information which would not be available without this push, they become convinced of the importance of confrontation and persistence.

Another form of confrontation occurs when I am convinced that the patient or family is not telling me the "whole truth" or leading me down the garden path. Often I get a fix on this when there is a disparity between the verbal and nonverbal messages. When this situation occurs, I confront the family with the discrepancies and tell them that I think they are not being truthful. I also use Fritz Perls' (1969) distinction between horseshit, bullshit, and elephantshit. In most cases, families respond quite well to the confrontation and vulgarity, as well as to my telling them that their little ploy will not work. Most families respect therapists who respond honestly and then offer the needed information.

DISTRACTIONS

I use "distractions" in treatment for basically two reasons: They keep me from being too bored and they insure that I do not get sucked into a family's emotional system or hypnotized or anesthetized by the family's style, depression, etc. There are several distracting things I have done for years in treatment sessions; let me mention just a couple.

When I first started my private practice, I saw individuals, couples, and families in my apartment, specifically in my living room, which also houses my baby grand piano. Every once in a while, during a session, someone would start giving me some hearts and flowers story, which prompted me to run to the piano and play some music appropriate to the story. This turned out to be a powerful distraction. The moment you play melodramatic music to a melodramatic story, the story loses some, if not all, of its power. This returns the control of the session to the therapist; moreover, it's funny, dramatic, and enlivening.

I also used to play the piano when I got bored in the session or when the patient passively waited until I took over. It's boring to simply wait until the patient gets bored with waiting, so I would entertain myself. Playing the piano for the few minutes or so between sessions also served as a cleansing or cathartic experience, at times permitting me to get rid of the feelings from a previous session, so I could be fresh for the next session.

Now that I have moved my office out of my home, I miss having my piano. The more I think about the importance of my piano in my treatment room, the more I think I will soon buy a small piano to place in my office.

Other distractions come from the technical aspects of videotaping treatment sessions. Normally I videotape most of the

treatment sessions in my private practice for three basic
reasons:

1) Since I am always experimenting with briefer forms of
   doing therapy, I need to study the sessions.
2) In the event I get stuck, I can always give the video-
   cassette of the last session to a colleague, who usually can get me unstuck in a few minutes.
3) Since I do a lot of training, I might want to use a session as a demonstration.

Videotaping requires a lot of technical toys, which are interesting distractions for me. For example, one of the things
I am most anxious about is the quality of the sound track of
the videotape. I usually have a sound mixer right next to me,
and periodically watch the sound meter so I know that I am
getting a good signal to noise ratio. Watching this meter
keeps me a little more outside the family's emotional system
than if there were no meter.

In addition, I have three videocameras and stay in a meta
position to the family by interesting myself in the quality of
the video which is being recorded while the session is being
conducted. During a family session, one of my video camera
people films the session and I am somewhat interested in
what shots are being taken, how the screen may be split, etc.
In other words, I am somewhat involved in directing what
shots are taken on the video, as well as conducting the family therapy session.

SUMMARY

This chapter has touched on some of the ways in which I
have tried to stay alive as a person and as a therapist. Many
of the ways of staying alive have to do with maximizing clinical leverage in various ways such as by maintaining meta
positions, varying time intervals within and between sessions,
and by avoiding the ways in which families can immobilize

therapists. The chapter also suggests that clinicians can and should use as much of themselves as they can in treatment sessions to stay alive while remaining effective as therapists. Some of the ways of using oneself in treatment include the strategic uses of humor, metaphor, confrontation, provocation and distraction.

REFERENCES

Bateson, G. (1972). *Steps to an ecology of mind*. New York: Ballantine Books.

Bergman, J. S. (1981, April) *Brief strategic interventions in family therapy*. Invited guest speaker at the convention of the American Academy of Psychoanalysis, Houston. (a)

Bergman, J. S. (1981, October) *Working without a team*. Presented at conference sponsored by the Ackerman Institute for Family Therapy, New York. (b)

Bergman, J. S. (1983). Prescribing family criticism as a paradoxical intervention. *Family Process, 22*(4), 517–522. (a)

Bergman, J. S. (1983). On odd days and on even days . . . Rituals used in strategic therapy. In B. Wolberg & E. Aronson (Eds.), *Group and family therapy* (pp. 273–281). New York: Brunner/Mazel. (b)

Bergman, J. S. (1983) *Using systems theory when working with couples and individuals*. Presented at conference sponsored by the Ackerman Institute for Family Therapy, New York. (c)

Bergman, J. S., & Walker, G. (1983) Anatomy of violence: A case study. In P. Papp (Ed.), *The process of change* (pp. 173–214). New York: Guilford.

Bergman, J. S. (1984, August) A proposal for the formation of a National Association for the Prevention of Cruelty to Couples. *Family Therapy News*.

Bloch, D. A. (1976). Including the children in family therapy. In P. Guerin (Ed.), *Family therapy: Theory and practice* (pp. 168–181). New York: Gardner Press.

Bowen, M. (1978). *Family therapy in clinical practice*. New York: Aronson.

Framo, J. L. (1981). The integration of marital therapy with sessions with family of origin. In A. S. Gurman & D. P. Kniskern (Eds.), *Handbook of family therapy* (pp. 133–158). New York: Brunner/Mazel.

Haley, J. (Ed.). (1967). *Advanced techniques of hypnosis and ther-*

apy: Selected papers of Milton H. Erickson. New York: Grune & Stratton.

Jackson, D. D. (Ed.). (1968). *Human communication, Vol. I, Communication, family, and marriage*. Palo Alto, Calif.: Science and Behavior Books.

LaPerriere, K. (1984) *Private practice*. Presented at conference of the American Family Therapy Association, New York.

Minuchin, S. (1974). *Families and family therapy*. Cambridge, MA: Harvard Press.

Morawetz, A., & Walker, G. (1984). *Brief therapy with single-parent families*. New York: Brunner/Mazel.

Palazzoli, M. Selvini (1978). *Couple therapy*. Fourth International Congress on Family Therapy, Florence, Italy.

Palazzoli, M. Selvini (1980). Why a long interval between sessions? The therapeutic control of the family-therapist suprasystem. In M. Andolfi & I. Zwerling (Eds.), *Dimensions of family therapy* (pp. 161–170). New York: Guilford.

Palazzoli, M. Selvini, Boscolo, L., Cecchin, G., & Prata, G. (1977). *Paradoxical approaches to family therapy*. Conference sponsored by the Ackerman Institute of Family Therapy, New York.

Palazzoli, M. Selvini, Boscolo, L., Cecchin, G., & Prata, G. (1978). *Paradox and counterparadox*. New York: Jason Aronson.

Papp, P. (Ed.). (1983). *The process of change*. New York: Guilford.

Perls, F. S. (1969). *Gestalt therapy verbatim*. Lafayette, CA: Real People Press.

Pittman, F. S., Flomenhaft, K., DeYoung, C., Kaplan, D. M., & Langsley, D. G. (1966). Techniques of family crisis therapy. In J. Masserman (Ed.), *Current psychiatric therapies*. New York: Grune & Stratton.

Simon, R. (1983). Still R. D. Laing after all these years. *Family Therapy Networker, 7*(3), 22.

Watzlawick, P., Weakland, J., & Fisch, R. (1974). *Change: Principles of problem formation and problem resolution*. New York: Norton.

Whitaker, C. (1972). Teachers and learners. In A. Ferber, M. Mendelsohn, & A. Napier (Eds.), *The book of family therapy*. Boston: Houghton Mifflin.

Whitaker, C. (1976). A family is a four-dimensional relationship. In P. Guerin (Ed.), *Family therapy: Theory and practice* (pp. 182–192). New York: Gardner Press. (a)

Whitaker, C. (1976). The hindrance of theory in clinical work. In P. Guerin (Ed.), *Family therapy: Theory and practice* (pp. 154–164). New York: Gardner Press. (b)

INDEX